BISHOPS' TRANSCRIPTS
AND
MARRIAGE LICENCES,
BONDS AND ALLEGATIONS

A Guide to their Location and Indexes

Fourth Edition

Compiled by Jeremy Gibson

Federation of Family History Societies

First published 1981 by the
Federation of Family History Societies.

Fourth edition published 1997 by
Federation of Family History Societies (Publications) Ltd., c/o The Benson Room,
Birmingham and Midland Institute, Margaret Street, Birmingham B3 3BS, England.

Second edition, 1982
Third edition, 1991

Fourth edition, Copyright © J.S.W. Gibson, 1997

ISBN 1 86006 053 6

Printed by Parchment (Oxford) Limited
from computer discs prepared by the editor

'All the Bishops courts are kept in each Citty, managed by Chancelours which are lay men, and the Suragats, also the Bishops deputyes, the Proctors, Parolers...; from hence are given out Licences for marriages...'

Celia Fiennes, writing about 1700.

Acknowledgments

A guide of this nature can only be compiled from information supplied by archivists and librarians, supplemented by existing reference works. When first compiling this Guide sixteen years ago I received the greatest assistance from archivists in county and diocesan record offices throughout England and Wales. For this new edition all record offices have once again been circulated and the response has as always been excellent. It is a pleasure to be able to thank my correspondents collectively, and it is my hope that the information provided here is up to date in every way, reflecting the continuing transcripton and indexing of these records.

Frequent reference is made throughout to the Society of Genealogists and to its invaluable series, the *National Index of Parish Registers*. County volumes continue to appear produced by dedicated series and individual editors, to whom all genealogists owe much. Lydia Collins' *Marriage Licences: abstracts and indexes in the library of the Society of Genealogists*, which has been through several editions, is another most useful catalogue, which will often provide further details of printed and other books mentioned briefly here.

J.S.W.G.

Federation of Family History Societies (Publications) Ltd. is a wholly owned subsidiary of
the Federation of Family History Societies, Registered Charity No. 1038721.

CONTENTS

INTRODUCTION

This is a guide to the location of Bishops' Transcripts and of the records connected with the issue of Marriage Licences. It also describes any abstracts, calendars and indexes to the latter, published or unpublished, and, when these are lacking, gives an indication of the arrangement of the surviving original documents. For Bishops' Transcripts, reference is given to any lists of parishes giving covering dates or more precise indication of exactly what years exist.

It is not my purpose to discuss the history or the content of these records, with which most users will be familiar before consulting this guide. They are described in genealogical textbooks, and in particular by Donald Steel in the *National Index of Parish Registers*, vol. 1 (1968), and by David E. Gardner and Frank Smith *in Genealogical Research in England and Wales*, vol.1 (1956).

The location of the two classes of records can be conveniently described together, as both were, like probate records, connected with ecclesiastical jurisdictions. As a result, both are usually, though not always, in the same diocesan record offices. However, apart from both being ecclesiastical records, they have no administrative connection. The arrangement of this guide, like others I have produced, is by the pre-1974 historic English and Welsh counties, as it is with these administrative areas that historians deal.

From the reign of Elizabeth I, **Bishops' Transcripts** (or Register Bills) were supposed to be returned annually, by the clergy of each parish, to the Bishop, archdeacon or peculiar authority. Their survival has varied widely, as described under each county heading. There is invariably a gap for the period of the Civil War and the Commonwealth (the 1640s and 1650s), as diocesan and similar authority was suspended or abolished at the time (and this is the case with Marriage Licence records too). It will be found that after the introduction of civil registration in 1837 only baptisms and burials are usually returned, and the submission of the transcripts, in general, died out in the later nineteenth century. It should always be borne in mind that the Bishops' Transcripts are likely to be a less than full copy of the actual registers, and where possible these should be consulted too.

Marriage Licences themselves will only survive by chance, as they were issued to the groom for presentation to the parson conducting the marriage. The records of use to historians are those that were retained in the issuing office, bonds, allegations and registers of licences. These may contain, variously, in addition to the names of groom and bride, the groom's occupation, places in which each lived and where the marriage was to take place, their ages (particularly if minors), and the names and occupations of bondsmen (often relatives). The exact details can be ascertained from the reference books mentioned, and, as in all historical records, information that should be given often may be found to be missing.

Marriage Licences were used by a wide social strata - not merely nobility and gentry, but by almost anyone with claims to standing above labouring class: moreover, until Lord Hardwicke's Act came into operation in 1754, it seems almost to have been customary, for those with such pretensions, to marry away from their home parishes, often in the neighbouring market or county town. Discovery of the appropriate Marriage Licence record may lead to one such a 'lost' marriage. But it should also be remembered that issue of a Licence did not mean that the marriage necessarily took place.

In this guide I have concentrated on giving information on the finding aids for Bishop's Transcripts and Marriage Licence records. For this new edition, sixteen years after its first appearance, all record offices have been freshly circulated and given the opportunity to update their entries. In general additions are limited to the increasing availability of the records in microform, and alterations to the constantly changing names of the repositories. For the first time county maps showing ecclesiastical jurisdictions are included, which save users having to consult the companion guide to *Probate Jurisdictions*.

Those requiring more precise details of the original records should consult volume 2 of *Genealogical Research in England and Wales* (1959); *A guide to Marriage Licences, Bonds and Allegations*, by Cecil Humphery-Smith (originally published in *Family History, 5, 25*, new series no. 1, January 1967); or the record office concerned. Lydia Collins' *Marriage Licences: Abstracts and Indexes in the Library of the Society of Genealogists* is also useful, though currently out of print. This has helped me to add references to a few minor published collections earlier overlooked and draw attention to some additional holdings in the Society's library. I am particularly grateful for permission to include details of published lists of Irish marriage licence records. Obviously anyone using the Society's library should consult this catalogue, which in places gives considerably more detail than space allows here.

Reference as appropriate has been made to volumes of the *National Index of Parish Registers* produced under various editorships. Hugh Peskett's guide to Devon and Cornwall registers, published by Devon and Cornwall Record Society in 1979, performs the same good service for those counties, as do a number of excellent record office guides elsewhere.

Archivists and librarians have been very helpful in answering my questionnaires and subsequent enquiries, as have users of earlier editions who have sent me corrections and additional information. I shall continue to be most grateful for any such that are brought to my notice.

J.S.W.G.
Harts Cottage,
Church Hanborough,
Witney,
Oxon. OX8 8AB.

ABBREVIATIONS

A	Allegations
A.S.	Archaeological Society
B.	Bonds
BT	Bishop's Transcripts
B.R.S.	British Record Society
c.	*circa* or about
C16 etc.	16 century *etc.*
F.H.S.	Family History Society
Harl. Soc.	Harleian Society
I.G.I.	International Genealogical Index (of the Genealogical Society of the Church of Jesus Christ of Latter-Day Saints)
Mge	Marriage
ML	Marriage Licence (or records relating to it)
MS	manuscript
p., pp.	page, pages
R.O.	Record Office
R.S.	Record Society
Soc. of Gen.	Society of Genealogists (14 Charterhouse Buildings, Goswell Road, London EC1M 7BA, tel. 0171 251 8790)
TS	typescript

ENGLAND and WALES

Bishop's Transcripts

As their name implies, these were returns to a Bishop (occasionally to an Archdeacon). There was no superior central authority (nor any equivalent return to the Archbishops, except as diocesans), so BTs are to be found only in record offices relating to specific localities, and are identified in the ensuing county sections.

Marriage Licences

On the other hand, Marriage Licences might be issued by the Archbishop of Canterbury, as Metropolitan and Primate, for any part of England and Wales; and by the Archbishop of York for any part of the northern Province of York (in addition to those issued by bishops, archdeacons and their surrogates, for their own ecclesiastical jurisdictions). For convenience, the Archbishop of York's ML records are described under the section on Yorkshire, page ??.

The records of marriage (and divorce) of the Archbishop of Canterbury in *Lambeth Palace Library* are described in an article in *The Genealogists' Magazine* (**20**.4, December 1980), by Melanie Barber. The Archbishop was responsible for four distinct series of allegations, two very large collections being of national relevance.

These were the **Faculty Office**, which could authorise a marriage in any parish in England and Wales; and the **Vicar General** of the Archbishop of Canterbury, who issued licences to marry in any parish within the Province of Canterbury.

It should be emphasised that the vast majority of these MLs, though emanating from such high authority, were still common licences, not 'special licences' as often erroneously stated. This is fortunate, as the name of the parish where the ceremony is to take place is invariably omitted in special licences, whereas it should be mentioned in common licences. The two categories are in any case calendared and bound in the same series.

Records of the **Faculty Office** and the **Vicar General** are, as mentioned, at:

Lambeth Palace Library, London SE1 7JU.

Faculty Office

Published:
Faculty Office Registers, 1534-1549, by D.S. Chambers, 1966. Contains brief details only of the few MLs for the period.

Allegations for MLs issued by the Faculty Office of the Archbishop of Canterbury at London, 1543-1869, extr. J.L.Chester, ed. G.J Armytage, Harleian Society **24** (1886). This is misleadingly titled, as in fact it only contains a complete coverage for the relatively few pre-1632 MLs:
1543-1549 (about 650); **1567-1575** (88).

Thereafter, the British Record Society **33** calendar ed. G.E. Cokayne and E.A. Fry (1905), for the period **1632-1714** (gap 1650-1660), should first be consulted. This lists all names, chronologically, with an index, but gives no other details. However, asterisked entries in this will be found in Harleian Soc. **24**, which though giving selected MLs only, does give full details of those, abode and parish of marriage *etc.*

A full name index from 2 August **1714** to **1850**, from microfilm of the MS calendars (in *Lambeth Palace Library*) is in process of compilation at the *Society of Genealogists*, to be published on fiche and possibly in hard copy.

This will shortly supersede the MS calendars, which list full names of each party in chronological order. To *c*.1837 there are 13 volumes to calendar 204 volumes of allegations. Microfilm of calendars to 1845 at the **Society of Genealogists** (5 reels), as well as film copies of the allegations themselves, **1715-1851**.

Vicar General (Province of Canterbury):

Published:
The records only survive from 1660, and between 1660 and 1679 there are alternative volumes to consult:
Allegations for MLs issued by the Vicar General... **1660-1679**, extr. J.L. Chester, ed. G.J. Armytage, Harleian Society **23** (1886); this volume is of extracts only, and those omitted were subsequently published as below:
    1660-1668 (Harl. Soc. **33**, 1892);
    1669-1679 (Harl. Soc. **34**, 1892).

Two further volumes contained all entries of the periods covered:
    1679 (July) - **1687** (June) (Harl. Soc. **30**).
    1687 (July) - **1694** (June) (Harl. Soc. **31**).
Each volume is arranged chronologically, with index of personal names, full details, including abode and place of marriage, being given.

A surname index **1701-1750** is in process of compilation at the Society of Genealogists.

1751-1850 published on fiche and in hard copy by the *Society of Genealogists*, 1997.

Unpublished:
    TS index: July **1694** - Dec. **1699**;
    Jan. **1700** - Dec. **1705**;
    Jan. **1706** - Dec. **1709**;
Alphabetical, grooms and brides in one sequence. Exact date shown for men; for women, year only, cross-refer to men for exact date. Personal names only, no places etc. Copy at *Society of Genealogists* (copies of 1694-1699 and 1706-1709 only, also at *Lambeth Palace Library*). The *Society of Genealogists* (14 Charterhosue Buildings, London EC1M 7BA) also has film copies of the full allegations from **1660** to **1851**; and for **1694-1707** and **1801-1803** in its card index.

England and Wales:
Vicar General continued

In contrast to the TS the cards give details of places.

The Society of Genealogists' indexes 1700-1850 effectively supersede the MS calendars at Lambeth Palace Library (and film of these elsewhere). Note that they include MLs for the deaneries of the peculiars of Canterbury: Shoreham (Kent, page 26); Croydon (Surrey, page 43, and Middlesex); and the Arches (London, page 31).

BEDFORDSHIRE

BTs and MLs for the entire county are at the

Bedfordshire Record Office, Bedford.

See the *National Index of Parish Registers*, **9**, part 1, 1991; and *Guide to the Bedfordshire Record Office*, 1957.

Bishop's Transcripts

Nearly all the county was in the **Archdeaconry of Bedford**, for which BTs run from 1602. They are arranged by parish for the 139 parishes, to 1849, thereafter chronologically.

There were two peculiars, for **Biggleswade** and **Leighton Buzzard**, with a few BTs separate but others in the main archdeaconry series.

Effectively all BTs for the county are transcribed to 1812 and all are published, as when the well-known series of Bedfordshire Parish Register transcripts were being prepared they were compared with the BTs and alternative readings and additional information incorporated. The Mormon I.G.I. has included baptisms and marriages from these published transcripts to 1812.

Marriage Licences

All surviving bonds and allegations for MLs to 1812 were published in the Bedfordshire Parish Register series vol. 14, **1747-1790**, and vol. 15, **1791-1812** (some big gaps prior to 1778, thereafter most survive to 1812). The few MLs for the **Leighton Buzzard Peculiar** are included in vol. 15. These are full abstracts, including both grooms and brides in the same alphabetical sequence with abode, date etc. A very few early entries from act books, 1578, 1610-11, 1616-18, are also included in vol. 15.

Original bonds and allegations continue to 1822, and allegations alone up to 1885. TS indexed calendars for ML allegations 1813-1885 are available at **Beds. R.O.** Indexed ML register 1813-85. Allegations 1822-23 are published in *Beds. F.H.S. Journal* **3**, 2 (Summer 1981), pp. 4-7.

A few Biggleswade peculiar ML records survive, 1714-1800, but are not apparently included in the published volumes.

Bedfordshire Notes & Queries **2** (1889), has extracts of entries relating to Bedfordshire people, mainly C16 and C17, from other printed sources.

See also **Faculty Office** and **Vicar General**'s ML records, pages 7 and 8.

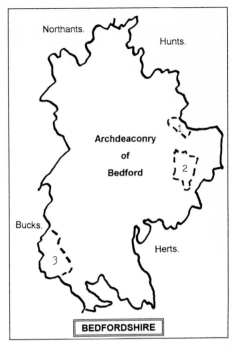

Places in Bedfordshire outside the jurisdiction of the archdeaconry (see map):
1. Everton (archdeaconry of Huntingdon)
2. Peculiar of Biggleswade
3. Peculiar of Leighton Buzzard:
   Leighton Buzzard and its former hamlets of
   Billington
   Eggington
   Heath and Reach
   Stanbridge

BERKSHIRE

(north-western Vale of the White Horse now in Oxfordshire)

The county formed the **Archdeaconry of Berkshire** in the **Diocese of Salisbury** until 1836, when it was transferred to the **Diocese of Oxford**.

Bishop's Transcripts

These are described in the *National Index of Parish Registers*, **8**, Part 1 (1989), which gives dates and location of surviving BTs for all parishes. They are also briefly listed in *Sources for Wiltshire Family History* (1997). A similar list for parishes now in Oxfordshire is in *Oxfordshire Parish Registers and BTs*, by C.G. Harris, Oxon. F.H.S., 5th ed., 1997.

Those before 1836 are at the

Wiltshire and Swindon Record Office, Trowbridge.

In general BTs date from the early C17, often one BT for 1607 followed by a more regular series from 1611 or 1614 to 1623, 1628, 1631, 1634-1637, and recommencing in the later 1660s.

The following parishes were in peculiars: Arborfield, Blewbury with Upton and Aston Upthorpe, Little Coxwell, Faringdon, Hungerford, Hurst, Ruscombe, Sandhurst, Sonning, Wantage, Wokingham. BTs survive from the 1580s or 1590s, with considerable gaps (for Little Coxwell, missing 1672-1812).

From 1836, BTs for Berkshire are at *Oxfordshire Archives, Oxford.*

Marriage Licences

Again, see the *National Index of Parish Registers*, **8**, Part 1 (1989). There were two main authorities for the issue of MLs, the **Bishop of Salisbury (Sarum)** and the **Archdeacon of Berkshire**.

The main diocesan series of bonds and allegations is at the *Wiltshire and Swindon Record Office*, and is complete from 1615 except for the Commonwealth period. These bonds and allegations have been fully abstracted to 1823, as detailed on page 46, under 'Wiltshire'. Despite the transfer of the Archdeaconry to the Diocese of Oxford in 1836, some bonds and allegations continue to occur in the Sarum series up to at least 1845.

Records of the **Peculiar of the Dean of Salisbury**, also at the *W. & S. R.O.*, include bonds and allegations from 1638 for Berkshire parishes in that peculiar: Arborfield, Blewbury with Upton and Aston Upthorpe, Hurst, Ruscombe, Sandford, Sonning and Wokingham. For details of abstracts etc., see under 'Wiltshire', page 47.

Bonds for Wantage (only), 1669-1693 (23 only) in the **Peculiar of the Dean and Canons of Windsor**, *W. & S. R.O.*, have been published in *The Oxfordshire Family Historian*, **3**, 2 (Summer 1983). Although there are no other ML records for the C18 or for other parishes in the Peculiar amongst records of the Peculiar, details of MLs for Wantage are also to be found in the Archdeaconry of Berkshire index (see below) 1616-38, 1669-79; and also for 1672 and 1674 (17) in a book amongst the Dean of Salisbury's material at *W. & S. R.O.* [D5/35, ff. 30-31, 45-46].

Berkshire parishes outside the jurisdiction of the archdeacon of Berkshire.

Peculiars: F - Faringdon; **S** - Dean of Salisbury; **W**- Dean and Canons of Windsor in Wantage.

Arborfield **S6**; Aston Upthorne **S3**; Blewbury **S3**; Little Coxwell **F1**; Great Faringdon **F1**; Hungerford **W5**; Hurst **S6**; West Ilsley **W4**; Ruscombe **S6**; Shalbourne (part Wilts.) **W5**; Sonning **S6**; Upton **S3**; Wantage **W2**; Wokingham **S6**.

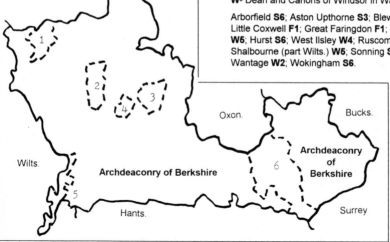

Berkshire: MLs continued

The original Marriage Bonds for the **Archdeaconry of Berkshire** were destroyed by enemy action in World War II. However, there is a C19 MS index to these lost bonds, 1616-1638, 1669-1846, copies at **Berkshire Record Office, W. & S. R.O., Oxon. Archives, Bodleian Library**, Oxford, and **Society of Genealogists**. This is arranged alphabetically by bridegrooms within each year, giving names and abodes of each party. Bonds for peculiars of **Faringdon** and **Langford** are listed at the end. In addition, there is a fully alphabetical card index of all brides and grooms in this C19 MS index, at the **Berkshire Record Office**, Reading,

For a description of the indexes to the Archdeaconry of Berkshire Bonds, see *Berkshire Family Historian* **5**, 2, or *The Oxfordshire Family Historian* **1**, 9 (Autumn 1979).

There is a list of MLs granted by the Archdeacon of Berkshire, 1826-1835, at **Berkshire R.O.** [D/A 2 c.173]. There is also has a slip index (by brides and grooms) of all MLs that chance to survive in **B.R.O.**

Bonds for the Berkshire peculiar of (Great) **Faringdon** (and Little Coxwell), 1664-1740, are now at the **Berkshire R.O.** [D/A 2 c.190-191]. Those for **Langford** (with Little Faringdon), 1676-1814, are now at **Oxfordshire Archives**. Both are included in the full TS abstract of bonds (arranged alphabetically) from peculiars formerly in the Bodleian.

See also **Faculty Office** and **Vicar General**'s ML records, pages 7 and 8.

BUCKINGHAMSHIRE
(southern tip now in Berkshire)

***Buckinghamshire Record Office**, Aylesbury*

has BTs (now microfilmed) for most and MLs for virtually all of the county. See leaflet *Notes for the Guidance of Genealogists.*

Bishop's Transcripts

Comprising those for the **Archdeaconry of Buckingham** (which was approximately co-terminous with the county), *c.1600-c.1840*; some formerly in the Lincoln diocesan records; and those for four parishes formerly in **St. Albans Archdeaconry**; a few BTs for these are also at **Guildhall Library**, pages 23 and 30 (Aston Abbots 1629-30, 1639-40; Grandborough 1629, 1639-40; Little Horwood 1629, 1639-40; Winslow 1629, 1639).

A detailed list, showing gaps, is published in *Bucks. Ancestry* **1** (Bucks. F.H.S., 1981), now superseded by *the National Index of Parish Registers*, **9**, part 3 (1992).. A consolidated catalogue at the **Buckinghamshire Record Office** gives references for each parish and shows missing years (2 vols.).

Buckinghamshire: BTs continued

BTs for parishes in peculiars, formerly at the Bodleian, are now at the **Bucks. R.O.** From *c.*1845 BTs for the archdeaconry are with the Oxford diocesan records **at Oxfordshire Archives**, Oxford. These mainly continue to 1874.

Exceptions:

BTs for former Oxon. parishes Lillingstone Lovell and Stokenchurch are at **Oxfordshire Archives**. BTs for the peculiar of Eton, for the parish of Eton only, were reputed to be at **Eton College**, but were not there in 1992.

Buckinghamshire parishes outside the jurisdiction of the archdeacon of Buckingham:

A: Archdeaconry of St. Albans
B: Peculiar of Bierton *(Bodleian)*
O: Diocese and Archdeaconry of Oxford
P: Other Peculiars *(Bucks. R.O.)*

Aston Abbots **A4**; Aylesbury **P6**; Bierton **B7**; Buckingham **P2**; Buckland **B9**; Caversfield (det.) **O**; Eton **14**; Granborough **A3**; Halton **P10**; Little Horwood **A3**; Ibstone or Ipstone **0-13**; Lillingstone Lovell **0-1**; Monks Risborough **P12**; Quarrendon **B5**; Stoke Mandeville **B8**; Stokenchurch **0-13**; Towersey **P11**; Winslow **A3**.

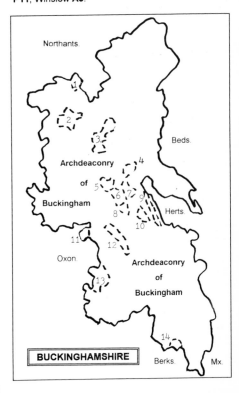

Marriage Licences

The bonds and allegations for the **Archdeaconry of Buckingham** and the various peculiars (except Eton) are fully available in an excellent 3 vol. TS. alphabetical abstract, 1663-1849 (few before 1733). This gives details of parties, place, age, occupation, omitting only names of persons other than the parties: indexes to brides at the end of each volume. Copies at **Bucks R.O., Oxfordshire Archives** and **Bodleian Library**, Oxford. This index also includes Oxon. peculiars.

For the **St. Albans Archdeaconry**, in the diocese of London, see also Herts., page 23, and London, page 30.

See also **Faculty Office** and **Vicar General**'s ML records, pages 7 and 8.

CAMBRIDGESHIRE

Most of the county was in the **Diocese of Ely**, for which BTs and MLs are at the

Ely Diocesan Records,
Cambridge University Library, Cambridge
(reader's ticket must be obtained on arrival).

A few parishes in the east were in the Archdeaconries of Sudbury or Norfolk, Diocese of Norwich.

Bishop's Transcripts

Location and extent of BTs for all parishes, with main gaps, are in *Genealogical Sources in Cambridgeshire* (Cambs R.O., 2nd edn. 1994) and the *National Index of Parish Registers*, **7** (1983). These also give details of modern transcripts and indicate if these have been checked with BTs. Most marriages from BTs have been included in Boyd's Marriage Index, but 1626-1675, and supplementary indexes for 1754-1837 (as well as a photocopy of Boyd's Index, 1538-1626, 1675-1837) are at the

County Record Office, Cambridge.

A series of modern transcripts is in progress and these generally include comparison with BTs. The Mormon I.G.I. includes many such modern transcripts.

Earlier guides: *Ely Episcopal Records* by A. Gibbons, 1891, and *Ely Records: A Handlist of the Records of the Bishop and Archdeacon of Ely*, Dorothy M. Owen, 1971, also give details of BTs (but note that BTs for the deaneries of Bourn, Shingay and Cambridge, 1783-1812, stated to be 'wanting', have now been found; dates given in the handlist are not all accurate, and c.50 unidentified BTs have now been identified and added to the series).

BTs for the diocese of Ely in general date from about 1599.

BTs for 14 parishes in **the Archdeaconry of Sudbury** are at the

Suffolk Record Office (Bury St. Edmunds branch), Bury St. Edmunds.

These are Ashley, Burwell, Cheveley, Chippenham, Exning, Fordham, Kennett, Kirtling, Landwade, Newmarket All Saints and St. Mary, Snailwell, Soham, Wicken, and Wood Ditton. Except for Landwade (1638-40 only) BTs for these parishes start in C16. See page 42 for details. Microfilms of BTs for all these parishes in Fordham deanery 1562-1641, 1663-99 are at the **County Record Office**, Cambridge.

BTs for 1782-3 (only) survive for Isleham (**Peculiar of Isleham and Freckenham**), also at **Bury St. Edmunds**. The main series for Isleham is with Ely Diocesan Records (above), 1675-1708, 1715-1779, 1781, 1785-1841 [EDR/L5/I].

The parishes of Outwell, Upwell, and Welney were in the **Archdeaconry of Norfolk**. BTs from 1691 (Welney 1725) are at **Norfolk Record Office**, page 33.

Marriage Licences

Registers of MLs 1562-C20 (gaps 1600-1604, 1621-1659) most with contemporary indexes. The earliest are fully calendared, 1562-1582 (Gibbons, pp. 154-84), 1582-1591 (*Northern Genealogist*, **1**, pp. 15-19, 73-78). In addition to this Bishop's series, the Archdeacon also granted MLs, for which there are registers from 1727 (see Owen, pp. 35-6, 74). Also bonds 1703-45 (incomplete), 1745-1875, 1934-1953.

Ely ML bonds in Peterborough diocesan records, 1698-1699/1700, are published in Cambs. F.H.S. *Journal* **3**, 3 (Aug. 1981), pp. 70-72.

For parishes in the **Archdeaconries of Norfolk** and **Sudbury**, see pages 33 and 42.

See also **Faculty Office** and **Vicar General**'s ML records, pages 7 and 8.

Cambridgeshire continued

Archdeaconry of Ely ('**7**' on map unless otherwise stated):

Cambridge (all parishes) **6**; Abington Pigotts; Bassingbourn; Bourn; Boxworth; Caldecote; Caxton; Cherry Hinton **6**; Conington; Croxton; Croydon cum Clopton; Elsworth; Eltisley; Gt and Lit Eversden; Fen Drayton; Fulbourn **6**; Gamlingay; Guilden Morden; Graveley; Haddenham **5**; East Hatley; Hatley St. George; Kingston; Knapwell; Litlington; Lolworth; Longstowe; Melbourn; Meldreth; Papworth St. Agnes and Everard; Shingay; Steeple Morden; Swavesey; Tadlow; Toft; Wendy with Shingay; Whaddon; Wilburton **5**.

Parishes outside the jurisdiction of the Consistory Court of Ely:

Archdeaconry of Sudbury, 4
Ashley cum Silverley; Burwell; Cheveley; Chippenham; Wood Ditton; Fordham; Kennett; Kirtling; Landwade; Newmarket All Saints; Snailwell; Soham; Wicken.

Archdeaconry of Norfolk, 2
Outwell, Upwell, Welney.

Peculiars of Isleham, 3, and Thorney, 1.

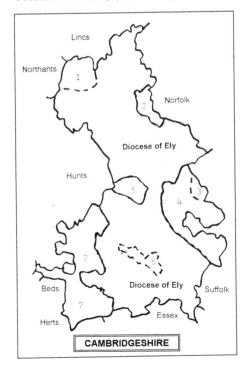

CAMBRIDGESHIRE

CHESHIRE
(northern border now in Greater Manchester; Wirral now in Merseyside)

Cheshire Record Office, Chester

has both BTs and MLs for whole of Cheshire, which was entirely within the **Diocese of Chester.**

Bishop's Transcripts

These are described in the *National Index of Parish Registers*, **10**, Part 1 (1995), which gives dates and location of surviving BTs for all parishes.

Occasional pre-1600; fairly regular from *c*.1606 on. No published list, but detailed TS list at **Cheshire Record Office**. Arranged by parish. Mainly available for consultation on microfilm.

Marriage Licences

Full abstracts (including abode and place of marriage) and indexes, 1606-1719, published by Lancashire and Cheshire Record Society:
from Act Books, 1605-31, 1639-44, 1661-1700 (vols. 53, 56, 57, 61, 65, 69, 73, 77; additional bonds and allegations may exist 1661-8, 1670-1700); bonds and allegations, 1700-1718/9 (vols. 82, 85, 97, 101). Abstracts 1719-1723 have been prepared for eventual publication.

From 1661 onwards the original bonds and allegations are arranged in chronological order. For 1716-1833 they are in alphabetical order by groom, annually. Bonds for 1776 (A-L only) are published in the F.H.S. of Cheshire *Journal*, (?1975-77). Arrangement chronological from (1834 at present. but these are in the process of being arranged in alphabetical order by groom, annually.

The records are for the **whole Archdeaconry of Chester**, which included Lancashire south of the Ribble, and the Flints. and Denbighs. parishes listed on page 53.

See also ML records of the Archbishop of York, page 49, and of the Faculty Office, page 7.

For a map of the county, see page 51.

CORNWALL

Cornwall formed the **Archdeaconry of Cornwall** in the **Diocese of Exeter**.

Bishop's Transcripts

These date from 1597. Dates of earliest and latest BTs are given in the *Guide to the Parish and Non-Parochial Registers of Devon and Cornwall, 1538-1837*, by Hugh Peskett (Devon and Cornwall Record Society, extra series, II, 1979; and Supplement, 1983), and are generally described on page xxxv. This includes details of parishes for which BTs may have been transcribed and published, along with parish registers. The Mormon I.G.I. will only include entries from such modern transcripts.

As a result of past administrative quirks BTs for the **Archdeaconry of Cornwall** are split anomalously: between

Devon Record Office, Exeter and
Cornwall County Record Office, Truro
(visits by appointment only):

1597-1673	Devon Record Office
1674-1736	Cornwall Record Office
1737-1740	Devon Record Office
1741-1772	Cornwall Record Office
1773-c.1850	Devon Record Office

All BTs held at *Devon Record Office* have been filmed, and microform copies for the whole county of those periods at the Devon Record Office are available at *Cornwall R.O.* and *Cornwall County Library (Cornish Studies Library)*, 2-4 Clinton Road, Redruth.

Similarly microform copies of all BTs at *Cornwall Record Office* are available at *Devon R.O., Exeter*.

BTs of parishes in **Bishop's** and **Dean and Chapter's Peculiars** are all at *the Devon Record Office* (with microform copies at *Cornwall R.O.*). These were: St. Agnes, St. Anthony in Roseland, Boconnoc with Bradoc, St. Breock, Budock, Egloshayle, St. Erney, St. Ervan, St. Eval, Falmouth, (St.) Germans, (St.) Gerrans, St. Gluvias, St. Issey, Landrake, Lawhitton, Lezant, Mabe, St. Merryn, Mylor, Padstow, Perranzabuloe, Little Petherick (or St. Petrock Minor), South Petherwin, Trewen and St. Winnow.

However, BTs for the **Royal Exempt Peculiar of St. Buryan** are all at the *Cornwall R.O.* (St. Buryan 1691, St. Levan 1694, Sennen 1699, all to 1847).

Marriage Licences

In general, see with Devon, page 16.

MLs for the **Peculiar of St. Germans**, 1704-1719/20, from act book, TS, by P.G. Peerless (1978) at *Society of Genealogists*.

CORNWALL

Devon

Arch-deaconry of Cornwall

CORNWALL

Parishes in peculiars:
B = Bishop of Exeter; **D** = Dean and Chapter of Exeter; **S** = St. Buryan.

St. Agnes **D5**; St. Anthony in Roseland **B7**; Boconnock with Bradoc **D3**; St. Breoke **B2**; Budock **B6**; (St.) Buryan **S8**; Egloshayle **B2**; St. Erney **B4**; St. Ervan **B2**; St. Eval **B2**; Falmouth **B6**; (St.) Germans **B4**; (St.) Gerrans **B7**; St. Gluvias **B6**; St. Issey **B2**; Landrake **B1**; Lawhitton **B1**; St. Levan **S8**; Lezant **B1**; Mabe **B6**; St. Merryn **B2**; Mylor **B6**; Padstow **B2**; Perranzabulo **D5**; Little Petherick (or St. Petroc Minor) **B2**; South Petherwyn **B1**; Sennen **S8**; Trewen **B1**; St. Winnow **D3**.

CUMBERLAND
(now part of Cumbria)

Cumbria Record Office, Carlisle

has BTs for the whole of the county except Alston, and MLs for the Diocese of Carlisle. See *Cumbrian Ancestors* (Cumbria Archive Service, 2nd edn. 1993, £4.99).

The greater part of Cumberland lay in the **Diocese of Carlisle**, but parishes south and west of the River Derwent were in **Diocese of Chester** (Archdeaconry of Richmond, Deanery of Copeland).

Bishop's Transcripts

Those for parishes in the **Diocese of Carlisle** date from about 1664, and those in the **Diocese of Chester** from about 1689. Starting and finishing dates (but not gaps) for all parishes are given in the *Cumbrian Ancestors*. Microfilm copies of all Cumberland BTs (except Alston) are also available at *Cumbria R.O., Kendal*.

BTs for the parish of Alston, which was in the Diocese of Durham, are at the *Durham University Library Archives and Special Collections, Durham*. See page 19 under 'Durham'.

Marriage Licences

There is a full typescript indexed calendar to marriage bonds for the **Diocese of Carlisle, 1668-1670, 1697-1824** (also supplement **1665-1671**) at the *Cumbria Record Office, Carlisle*, though the originals no longer survive. Those for **1668-1739** are published by Cumbria FHS, 1996. There are also registers of licences issued at Carlisle for all Cumberland and Westmorland parishes, 1860-1948 (surnames only, no locations).

For parishes in the **Archdeaconry of Richmond (Diocese of Chester)**, ML records are at *Lancashire Record Office, Preston*. Abstracts and indexes, 1648-1755, have been published by the Lancashire and Cheshire Record Society (vols. 74, 75, 80, 81, 83, 100, 115).

See also ML records of the **Archbishop of York**, page 49, and of the **Faculty Office**, page 7.

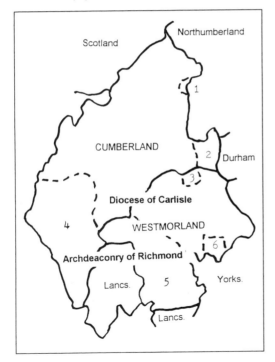

Parishes outside the jurisdiction of the consistory court of Carlisle:

Archdeaconry of Richmond, diocese of Chester:

Cumberland (Deanery of Copeland), 4
Arlecdon, Beckermet St. Bridget and St. John, Bootle, Brigham, Buttermere, Cleator, Clifton, Cockermouth, Corney, Dean, Distington, Drigg, Egremont, Embleton, Ennerdale, Eskdale, Gosforth, Harrington, Hensingham, Irton, Lamplugh, Lorton, Loweswater, Millom, Moresby, Mosser, Muncaster, Ponsonby, St. Bees, Setmurthy, Thwaites, Ulpha, Waberthwaite, Wasdalehead, Nether Wasdale, Whicham, Whitbeck, Whitehaven, Workington, Wythop.

Westmorland (deaneries of Kendal and Lonsdale), 5
Ambleside, Barbon, Beetham, Burnside, Burton in Kendal, Casterton, Crook, Crosthwaite, Firbank, Grasmere, Greyrigg, Holme, New and Old Hutton, Hutton Roof, Hugill (Ings), Kendal, Kentmere, Killington, Kirby Lonsdale, Langdale, Mansergh, Middleton, Preston Patrick, Rydal, Selside, Long Sleddale, Over Staveley, Troutbeck, Underbarrow, Windermere, Winster, Witherslack.

Diocese of Durham, Alston with Garrigill, Cumb., **2**: Upper Denton, Cumb., **1**.

Peculiar of Ravenstonedale, 6
Peculiar of Temple Sowerby, 3.

DERBYSHIRE
See with Staffordshire, page 40.

DEVON

Devon was in the **Diocese of Exeter**, and original BTs for the county and most ML records for the diocese are at the

Devon Record Office, Exeter.

Bishop's Transcripts

These date from 1597. Dates of earliest and latest BTs are given in the *Guide to the Parish and Non-Parochial Registers of Devon and Cornwall, 1538-1837*, by Hugh Peskett (Devon and Cornwall Record Society, extra series, II, 1979; and supplement, 1983), and are generally described on page xxxv. This includes details of parishes for which BTs may have been transcribed and published, along with parish registers. The Mormon I.G.I. will only include entries from such modern transcripts.

The *Devon R.O., Exeter* has TS lists of parishes showing missing years (mainly for C17).

The BTs to 1812 have all been filmed, and microfilms for all parishes in the county are now available at the *West Devon Area R.O., Plymouth, West Devon Library, Plymouth,* and the *North Devon Record Office, Barnstaple,* as well as at the *Devon R.O., Exeter.*

Post-1812 original BTs are at Exeter only.

Devon continued

Marriage Licences

There are 20 volumes of calendars and indexes to ML records of the **Diocese of Exeter**, 1523-1837, in the library of the Devon and Cornwall Record Society. This is housed in the *Westcountry Studies Library, Exeter,* in the same building as the *Devon Record Office.* Temporary membership of the Society, with use of its library, is available on the spot for a modest sum.

The earliest calendar, **1579** (with a few earlier entries, and a hiatus 1598-1609) to **1631**, by J.L. Vivian, is printed, but the index is a separate TS (also available at the *Society of Genealogists*). See also additions to Vivian, 1598-1599, in *Devon and Cornwall Notes and Queries,* **10** (1918-19), pp.321-26. The remaining volumes are TS, and initially may be confusing and seemingly overlapping. The library staff should be consulted as to their best use. The *Society of Genealogists* has copies of these: from act books, 1631-42, 1644, 1661-68 (indexed); 1668-1762 (10 vols.); from allegations, 1727-1733; index to allegations, 1660-1733.

The original records are at *Devon R.O.*

See also **Faculty Office** and **Vicar General**'s ML records, pages 7 and 8.

16

DORSET

From 1542 to 1836 Dorset formed the **Archdeaconry of Dorset** in the **Diocese of Bristol**. The registry of the Bishop for the archdeaconry was in Blandford and all early records, including BTs and perhaps MLs, were destroyed by fire in 1731.

In 1836 the archdeaconry was transferred to the **Diocese of Salisbury**, and thus BTs and ML records are at the

Wiltshire and Swindon Record Office, Trowbridge.

Bishop's Transcripts

These are briefly described in *Sources for Wiltshire Family History* (1997). A consolidated list of all parishes in Dorset, including the many peculiars, showing covering dates and gaps of more than 2-3 years, is available in the search room. This replaces an earlier series of TS duplicated lists.

For most of the county BTs only exist from 1731 or 1732. They are arranged by parish to 1846, and thereafter are bound into yearly volumes.

However, a large number of parishes were in peculiars. For those in **'Sarum peculiars'**, listed below, BTs survive from the late C16 or very early C17 (except as indicated). The parishes (all in the **Peculiar of the Dean of Salisbury** except those asterisked) were:

Alton Pancras, Anderson, Beaminster*, Bere Hackett, Bere Regis, Bloxworth, Castleton, Caundle Marsh, Chardstock*, Charminster, Clifton Maubank (BTs missing), Nether and Over Compton, Folke, Fordington*, Halstock*, Haydon, Hermitage, Holnest, Lillington, Long Burton, Lyme Regis*, Mapperton, Netherbury*, Oborne, Preston and Sutton Poyntz*, Ryme Intrinsica (from 1631), Sherborne, Stockwood, Stratton with Grimstone, Thornford, Turners Puddle, Wambrook*, Winterbourne Kingston, Winterbourne Thompson (from 1637, and very few throughout), North Wootton, Yetminster with Leigh and Chetnole*.

Another group of parishes were peculiars of the **Bishop of Bristol**, and for these BTs only survive from 1813:

Canford Magna with Kinson, Corfe Mullen, Hamworth, Lytchett Minster, Poole St. James, Sturminster Marshall, Wimborne Minster.

There are microfilm copies of all Dorset BTs for Bristol (later Salisbury) Diocese (at **Dorset Record Office**, *Dorchester.*

Marriage Licences

Bonds and allegations for the **Archdeaconry of Dorset** only appear to survive from 1798. The records are at the *Wiltshire and Swindon Record Office* and full abstracts have been made to 1832. They are, however, relatively few in number. As the archdeaconry was (until 1836) in the Diocese of Bristol, Dorset MLs do not occur in the Bishop of Salisbury's records.

For parishes in the **Peculiar of the Dean of Salisbury** (listed left), and for Stockland, in the **Peculiar of the Dean and Chapter**, see under 'Wiltshire', page 47, for details of ML records and abstracts at the *W. & S. R.O.*

For the **Peculiar of Gillingham** (including Motcombe), there are original bonds and allegations 1664-66, 1672, 1674, 1698-1729, 1745-1816 (not abstracted).

Abstracts of MLs for the **Royal Peculiar of Corfe Castle**, 1602-1800, are published in British Record Society **22**.

See also **Faculty Office** and **Vicar General**'s ML records, pages 7 and 8.

See overleaf for a map of the county.

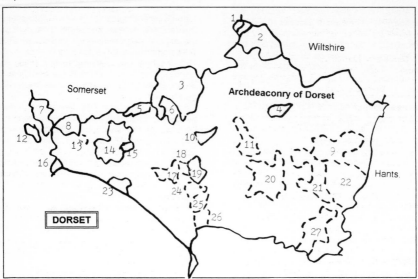

Parishes in Dorset in jurisdictions other than the archdeaconry of Dorset:

Note: records of the prebends of Chardstock, Lyme Regis and Halstock, Netherbury in ecclesia, Preston and Sutton Poyntz, and Yetminster and Grimston are to be found also in the peculiar court of the dean of Salisbury (in addition to the parishes in the direct jurisdiction of that court). Places in the liberty of Frampton also appear in the archdeaconry and consistory records.

BB : Burton Bradstock; **C** : Chardstock; **CC** : Corfe Castle; **CP** : Gt. Canford and Poole; **DC** : Dean and Chapter of Salisbury; **DS** : Dean of Salisbury; **E** : Diocese of Exeter; **F** : Frampton; **FW** : Fordington and Writhlington; **G** : Gillingham; **LR** : Lyme Regis and Halstock; **MA** : Milton Abbas; **N** : Netherbury; **P:** Preston and Sutton Poyntz; **SM** : Sturminster Marshall; **ST** : Stratton; **WM** : Wimborne Minster; **Y** : Yetminster and Grimston.

Alton Pancras **DS10**; Anderson **DS20**; Beaminster **N&DS14**; Bere Hacket **DS3**; Bere Regis **DS20**; Bettiscombe **F13**; Bincombe **F25**; Bloxworth **DS20**; Bourton **G1**; Burton Bradstock **BB23**; Gt Canford **CP22**; Castleton **DS3**; Caundle Marsh **DS3**; Chardstock **C&DS7**; Charminster **DS19**; Chetnole **Y&DS6**; Clifton Maybank **DS3**; Nether Compton **DS3**; Over Compton **DS3**; Compton Valence **F17**; Corfe Castle **CC27**; Corfe Mullen **SM21**; Dalwood (archd. of Dorset, detd.) **12**; Folke **DS3**; Fordington **FW24**; Frampton **F17**; Grimston **Y18**, Halstock **LR&DS5**; Hamworthy **SM21**; Haydon **DS3**; Hermitage **DS3**; Holnest **DS3**; Kingston **CC27**; Leigh **Y&DS6**; Lillington **DS3**; Longburton **DS3**; Lyme Regis **LR&DS16**; Lytchett Minster **SM21**; Mapperton **DS15**; Milborne Stileham **DS20**; Milton Abbas **MA11**; Motcombe **G2**; Netherbury **N&DS14**; Oborne **DS3**; Poole **CP22**; Preston **P26**; Ryme Intrinsica **DS3**; Sherborne **DS3**; Stockland (archd. of Dorset, detd.) **12**; Stockwood **DS3**; Stourpaine **DC4**; Stratton **ST&DS18**; Sturminster Marshall **SM21**; Sutton Poyntz **P&DS26**; Thorncombe **E8**; Thornford **DS3**; Tomson **DS20**; Turners Puddle **DS20**; Wambrook **C&DS7**; Wimborne Minster **WM9**; Winterborne Came **F25**; Winterborne Herringstone **F25**; Winterborne Kingston **DS20**; Winterborne Tomson **DS20**; Woolland **MA11**; North Wootton **DS3**; Yetminster **Y&DS6**.

DURHAM and NORTHUMBERLAND

Apart from the Peculiar of Hexamshire (see below) the two counties were entirely within the Diocese of Durham. BTs and MLs for the diocese are at the

Durham University Library Archives and Special Collections, Palace Green Section, Durham.

Bishop's Transcripts

These date from about 1760 to the mid C19, arranged by parish, with a Summary List of outside dates in *Durham Diocesan Records: BTs of PRs* (2nd ed., 1982, updated 1986 and 1991, available from the University at the above address). The *National Index of Parish Registers* **11** (Part 1), 2nd ed. (1984), gives similar information. Occasional pre-1758 BTs survive only for Durham St. Nicholas, Heddon on the Wall, Kirkwhelpington, Newcastle St. John and Bishopwearmouth.

BTs to 1837 for the Peculiar of Hexham and Hexhamshire, in Northumberland (Hexham, Allendale and St. John Lee, from 1740; Ninebanks,1767; Whitley, 1765, and chapelries) are at the *Borthwick Institute*, York (page 49; see Borthwick Institute *Handlist of Parish Registers Transcripts*, N.K.M. Gurney, 1976), with microfilm copies at *Hexham Library*. Most surviving post-1837 BTs for these places are at Durham.

All the known surviving BTs for the **Peculiar of Thockrington** are at *Durham*.

Marriage Licences

Bonds effectively survive from 1664 though there are a few earlier strays. Bonds and allegations are in yearly bundles covering the whole diocese and in approximate date order (card index of persons 1817-1820).

TS calendar, 'Durham Marriage Bonds 1590-1815', by E. Dodds and J.W. Robinson, in 14 vols., each indexed, at *Newcastle* and *Sunderland Central Libraries*. The volume 1686-1754 has separate indexes for men and women, but the remainder have composite indexes. Microfilm copies of this calendar are at the *Durham University Library Archives and Special Collections, Northumberland R.O.* and *Gateshead Library*.

There is also a printed volume, *Durham Marriage Bonds 1664-1674* (1912) fully indexed; and details of 220 bonds 1662-1666 in *The Northern Genealogist* (1895 and 1896).

Durham Diocesan Records Marriage Bonds cover *c.*1664 (with a few earlies examples) to 1823, after which date they were no longer required. Allegations cover *c.*1738 - C20 (permission from Diocesan Registrar needed to consult allegations less than 60 years old).

For the **Peculiar of Hexham and Hexhamshire** there is one box of bonds, 1704-1743, at the *Borthwick Institute* (indexed).

See also ML records of the **Archbishop of York**, page 49, and of the **Faculty Office**, page 7.

For a map, see page 51.

ESSEX

Most records of BTs and MLs are at the **Essex Record Office,** *Chelmsford.*

Bishop Transcripts

These are only extant for 1800-1878 and all parishes are deficient 1810-12.

Peculiars: Hornchurch 1770-1864; Sokens 1813-1877; Writtle 1813-38; Good Easter 1814-1866.

The only earlier BTs to survive are for the years 1629-30 (Willingale Doe, 1626-28 also), and 1638-39, for about 200 Essex parishes. These are in *Guildhall Library, London.* They have all been transcribed by S.W. Prentis, copies *at Guildhall Library, Essex Record Office, Chelmsford,* and the *Society of Genealogists.*

There are also odd years, mainly 1706 and 1715, for about 16 parishes, also transcribed by Prentis.

Marriage Licences

Records for various Essex jurisdictions are at the *Essex Record Office, Chelmsford,* from 1665 to the mid-C19. An index to most if not all of these records originally compiled by R.H. Browne in 1903 was computerised by John Rayment and a fully alphabetical print-out to grooms' names is at the *E.R.O., Chelmsford* and *Colchester,* the *Society of Genealogists* and the *Institute for Heraldic and Genealogical Studies, Canterbury.* The peculiars are indexed separately.

A similar index in calendar form (F.A. Crisp MSS), including MLs no longer extant, is at *Colchester Library (Local Studies)* (m'f at *E.R.O., Chelmsford*).

TS of MLs from act books, **Commissary of London for Essex and Herts.**, 1619-1669, **Archdeaconry of Colchester,** 1585-1641, **Archdeaconry of Essex,** 1579-1640, at *Essex R.O., Chelmsford,* and the *Society of Genealogists.*

Records of Essex MLs may also appear in the main Diocese of London series at *Guildhall Library,* see page 30.

Barling, Belchamp St. Paul's, Heybridge, Navestock, Tillingham, Wickham St. Paul's, were in the **Peculiar of the Dean and Chapter of St. Paul's,** 1670-1840, ML records now at *Guildhall Library.*

Bocking, Borley, Little Coggeshall, Latchingdon, Southchurch, Stisted, Runsell in Danbury, and Milton in Prittlewell were in the **Peculiar of the Archbishop of Canterbury in the Peculiar Deanery of Bocking.** Marriage allegations and bonds, 1771-1831, calendared and indexed (TS in preparation), are at *Lambeth Palace Library.*

St. Mary Maldon was in **the Peculiar of the Dean and Chapter of Westminster,** page 31.

ML records for the **Peculiar of Hornchurch,** 1746-1841 (235), are at *New College,* Oxford.

See also **Faculty Office** and **Vicar General**'s ML records, pages 7 and 8.

Parishes in Essex outside the main jurisdiction of the commissary court of London (Essex & Herts div.) and the archdeaconries of Colchester, Essex and Middlesex:

L = commissary court of London (London div.); *Peculiars:* **B** = Bocking; **GE** = Good Easter; **P** = dean and chapter of St.Paul's; **S** = Sokens; **W** = Writtle with Roxwell; **Z** = dean and chapter of Westminster (not marked on map).

Barling **P14**; Belchamp St.Pauls **P1**; Bocking **B3**; Borley **B**; Chingford **L11**; Chrishall **Z**; Little Coggeshall **B**; Good Easter **GE5 & Z**; Epping **L11**; Heybridge **P6**; Kirkby-le-Soken **S4**; Latchingdon **B10**; Leyton **L11**; Loughton **L11**; Maldon St. Mary **Z**; Milton in Prittlewell **B15**; Navestock **P12**; Nazeing **L11**; Newport **Z**; Roxwell **W7**; Runsell in Danbury **B8**; Southchurch **B15**; Stisted **B3**; Thorpe-le-Soken **S4**; Tillingham **P9**; Waltham Holy Cross **L11**; Walthamstow **L11**; Walton-le-Soken **S4**; Wickham St. Paul's **P2**; Woodford **L11**; Writtle **W7**.

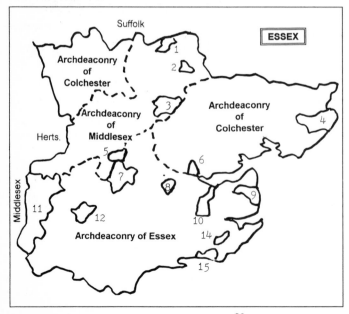

GLOUCESTERSHIRE and BRISTOL

For a general guide, see *Gloucestershire Family History*, by M.E. Richards (Glos. C.C., 3rd ed. 1993).

Most of Gloucestershire was in **the Diocese of Gloucester**, but the City of Bristol (comprising 17 parishes) and a few neighbouring parishes were in the **Diocese of Bristol**. BTs and MLs for the two dioceses are at the respective diocesan record offices, except for some southern Gloucester diocese parishes (listed below) whose BTs are at *Bristol*.

There are published lists of BTs deposited at the **Gloucestershire R.O.**, 1569-1812, and the **Bristol R.O.**, available from the respective offices. The *National Index of Parish Registers* **5** (1966), lists all parishes and shows changes of county or diocese; with starting dates of BTs in Gloucester diocese and full details and gaps of BTs in Bristol diocese. See also the very detailed *Guide to the Parish Records of the City of Bristol and the County of Gloucester*, ed. I. Gray and E. Ralph, Bristol and Glos. Arch. Soc., 1966. This also lists modern printed and MS transcripts, but not BTs.

Bishop's Transcripts

For the Diocese of Gloucester these are at the

Gloucestershire Record Office, Gloucester
(daily charge).

They date generally from 1598 but a few as early as 1569; then c.1607, a few mid-1610s, a fair number in 1620s, very few 1630s; 1660-1680, often a few missing, fairly complete then to 1812. In parish bundles to 1812.

From 1813 to c.1860, a full series, on microfilm, arranged by year, and then by parish,

There were several peculiars in the Diocese of Gloucester. In general BTs for these are not significantly less than normal, except for **Bibury** (incl. Aldsworth, Barnsley and Winson), for which there are very few pre-1813 BTs.

Parishes once in the Diocese of Gloucester, whose BTs are elsewhere, are listed below.

For the **Diocese of Bristol** BTs are at

Bristol Record Office, Bristol.

The following parishes originally formed the **Diocese of Bristol**, in general with BTs dating from 1660s/1670s: Almondsbury, Alveston, Bristol (all parishes), Clifton, Compton Greenfield, Elberton, Filton, Henbury, Horfield, Littleton-on-Severn, Mangotsfield, Olveston, Stapleton, Stoke Gifford, Westbury-on-Trym, Winterbourne St. Michael; also Abbots Leigh (Som.).

To these were added St. George, (formed 1756), Bedminster (Som.) (transferred 1837, BTs from 1598 to 1812; 1813-30 at *Somerset R.O.*) and Brislington (Som.) (transferred 1927, BTs from 1606).

In addition BTs to 1812 from the following Gloucester diocese parishes are at the **Bristol R.O.** Periods covered as for other Gloucester diocese parishes (see above), but post-1812 BTs are at the **Gloucestershire Record Office:** Cold Ashton, Bitton (incl. Hanham, Kingswood, Oldland), Dodington, Doynton, Dyrham (incl. Hinton), Frampton Cotterell, Iron Acton, Marshfield, Pucklechurch (incl. Abson and Wick), Siston, Tormarton (incl. West Littleton), Wapley (incl. Codrington), Westerleigh.

For BTs for Sutton-under-Brailes, to 1812, see **Warwicksire C.R.O.**, page 00; for Chaceley, *see* **Worcs. R.O.**, page 00.

Places in the jurisdiction of the **Consistory Court of Bristol**:

All parishes in the city of **Bristol**;
the **Gloucestershire** parishes of: Almondesbury, Alveston, Clifton, Compton Greenfield, Elberton, Filton, Henbury, Horfield, St.George Bristol, Littleton-on-Severn, Mangotsfield, Olveston, Stapleton, Stoke Gifford, Westbury-on-Trym, Winterbourne St.Michael; and Abbots Leigh (Som.); Bedminster (Som.) (from 1845 only).

Peculiars:
Bibury, 3: Aldsworth, Barnsley, Bibury, Winson.
Bishops Cleeve, 1: Bishops Cleeve, Stoke Orchard.
Withington, 2: Dowdeswell, Withington.

Note. Shenington, formerly in Glos., now in Oxon. was in the diocese of Gloucester until 1837 when it was transferred to the diocese of Worcester.

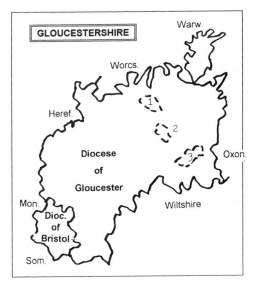

Gloucestershire and Bristol: BTs continued

There are modern copies of Marriages in BTs of a number of parishes in both dioceses. Information on these and their indexes (as at 1966) is given in the *National Index of Parish Registers* **5**. It is important to read the description of these on pp. 7-10. Later transcripts were given to *Gloucestershire R.O.* on Mr Roe's death in 1977.

Marriage Licences

As for BTs, records are in the diocesan record offices at Gloucester and Bristol. See *Gloucestershire Family History*, pp. 14-17; *National Index of Parish Registers* **5**, pp. 10-11.

For **Gloucester** diocese, there are two volumes of *Gloucestershire Marriage Allegations*, ed. B. Frith, Bristol and Glos. Arch. Soc. Records vols. 2, **1637-1680**, and 9, **1681-1700**. These are full abstracts, chronological and indexed.

Further court books containing notes of MLs 1640-1650, 1668-1676, have since been discovered.

Allegations 1701-1823 card indexed. Index to separate series of surrogates' allegations in progress.

There is also a MS copy and index of allegations and grants of MLs 1637, 1638, 1660-1753 at the *Society of Genealogists*.

Original allegations are in two series, those sworn before surrogates [Q2] and those sworn in the diocesan court [Q3]. The Q3 series is card indexed, 1700-1823. The series itself is bound in annual volumes some of which have their own name index. The Q2 series is indexed, and consists of loose leaves arranged roughly in 6-monthly bundles. There are also two index volumes to MLs issued 1830-1854, 1876-1906.

The references in the *National Index of Parish Registers* **5**, pp. 2-3 and 10, to allegations and bonds listed in the Gloucester City Library catalogue are incorrect, and do in fact relate to Roe's marriage indexes, based on parish registers and BTs, but not MLs, now in the *Gloucestershire Record Office*.

For **Bristol** diocese, abstracts and indexes are published in *Marriage Bonds for Diocese of Bristol, 1637-1700*, by D. Hollis (Bristol and Glos. Arch. Soc. **1** (1952). This supersedes the earlier volume by Fry. MS annual chronological indexes 1700-1800 (British Record Soc.) at the *Bristol Record Office*. ML registers from 1750 (card index, 1804-27), also bonds and allegations in annual bundles.

See also **Faculty Office** and **Vicar General**'s ML records, pages 7 and 8.

HAMPSHIRE
(Bournemouth area now in Dorset; Isle of Wight now a separate county)

Hampshire (including the Isle of Wight) was wholly in the diocese of Winchester. Although there were many peculiars, these do not affect the arrangement of BT and ML records, so no county map showing these is necessary.

Hampshire Record Office, Winchester

has BTs and MLs for whole county (including the Isale of Wight). See leaflet *Sources for Genealogy*.

Bishop's Transcripts

These survive generally from 1780 (with some earlier examples) to dates between 1858 and 1897 (mostly 1860s and 1870s). Arranged by parish. Now on microfilm. Modern MS copies of all parishes to 1812 at the *Institute of Heraldic and Genealogical Studies, Canterbury*.

For Plaitford, Damerham, Martin, formerly Wiltshire, see *Wiltshire & Swindon R.O.*, page 46.

Marriage Licences

Abstracts and indexes have been published to records dated between 1607 and 1837:

1607-1640, ed. A.J. Willis, 1957, 1960;
1669-1680, ed. A.J. Willis, 1963;
1689-1693, 1701-1711, 1713-1837, ed. W.J.C. Moens, Harleian Society **35**, **36**, 1893. These are alphabetical, by grooms, with index to brides. Supplement to Harleian Society vols. in *Genealogists' Magazine* **14**, 2 and 3 (June/Sep. 1962), pp. 48-55, 73-82. The 1689-1837 Harleian Society volumes together with Supplement are available on microfiche (£5 include. p&p) from *Hampshire Record Office*. The allegations themselves, 1699-1901, have been microfilmed.

From 1838 marriage allegations are bundled by year. There are also volumes recording the issue of MLs, 1851-1983 in the Diocesan collection [21M65/E14/1-11].

For MLs of former Wiltshire parishes, see ML records at *Wiltshire & Swindon Record Office*.

See also **Faculty Office** and **Vicar General**'s ML records, pages 7 and 8.

HEREFORDSHIRE
(now part of Hereford and Worcester)

Virtually all of Herefordshire was in the **Diocese of Hereford**, for which records are now at the

Hereford Record Office, Hereford.

Bishop's Transcripts

Starting dates and all gaps to 1812 are shown in the *National Index of Parish Registers* **5** (1966).

The majority start about 1660 and continue until at least the 1860's, some later. The arrangement is by parish throughout.

Eight parishes in the south-west of the county were in the **Diocese of St David's** with records at the *National Library of Wales, Aberystwyth.* Parishes were Clodock (1687), Dulas (1818), Ewyas Harold (1700), Llancillo(1707), Michaelchurch Eskley (1687), Rowlston (1702), St. Margaret (1714), and Walterstone (1712). See page 53.

Marriage Licences

For the **Diocese of Hereford**, these are at the *Hereford Record Office.* Marriage bonds, 1661-1831, are on files in boxes; licence books, 1663-1787, are bound with contemporary indexes. Also allegations, 1663-1696, and returns of licences, 1709-1843. Allegations, 1834-1909, bound and indexed. Modern index to Marriage Bonds 1696-1710 only.

ML records for the **Diocese of St David's** are, like the BTs, at the *National Library of Wales.* From 1661, few for C17 or early C18. See page 53.

See also **Faculty Office** and **Vicar General**'s ML records, pages 7 and 8.

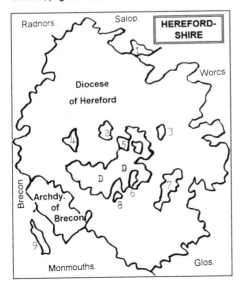

HERTFORDSHIRE

BTs and MLs for the Archdeaconries of St. Albans and Huntingdon (Hitchin division), which together covered much of the county, are held at the

Hertfordshire Archives and Local Studies, County Hall, Hertford.

Source leaflets available (for purchase) listing parish registers, BTs and nonconformist records at Hertford.

Bishop's Transcripts

Archdeaconry of St. Albans (St. Albans, most parishes to the south and 7 to the north, and Northaw - 22 in all). Fairly complete c.1570-1600. C17 very sketchy. Further gaps in first half of C18. BTs continue to c.1870 for some parishes, others end c.1850.

Archdeaconry of Huntingdon (Hitchin Div.) (remainder of county apart from exceptions below). From 1604, none for 1649-1660, gaps late C17 and early C18. Most parishes continue to 1870.

Most eastern border parishes were in the **Archdeaconry of Middlesex:**
Great Amwell, Anstey, Barkway, Barley, Braughing, Broxbourne, Buckland, Cheshunt, Eastwick, Gilston, Much and Little Hadham, Hoddesdon, Great and Little Hormead, Hunsdon, Layston, Meesden, Reed, Royston, Sawbridgeworth, Standon, Stanstead Abbots, Stanstead St. Margarets, Stocking Pelham, Bishops Stortford, Thorley, Thundridge, Ware, Widford, Wormley, Wyddial.
BTs from 1800 only are at *Hertfordshire Archives and Local Studies.* See below, *Guildhall Library,* for only earlier survivals.

BTs for the three Herts. parishes in the **Peculiar of the Dean and Chapter of St. Paul's** are also at the *Hertfordshire Record Office:*
Albury 1813-65; Brent Pelham 1829-1830; Furneux Pelham 1829-1831. None earlier.

BTs, mainly 1629-30 and 1639-40, survive for 36 Hertfordshire parishes at *Guildhall Library, London.*

Marriage Licences

Effectively all MLs from all surviving records are probably indexed in the Allen Marriage Index at the *Hertfordshire Archivves and Local Studies.*
There are also calendars published in *Hertfordshire Genealogist and Antiquary* (3 vols., 1895-1898) by William Brigg, and a separate alphabetical list by T.F. Allen for those not in Brigg:
Archdeaconry of St. Albans: Brigg, 1583-1715; Allen, 1715-1830;
Archdeaconry of Huntingdon, Hitchin division: Brigg 1610-1649; Allen, 1682-1685, 1756-1837.
The two gaps in the Archdeaconry of Huntingdon are gaps in the originals. Early entries in both series are taken from the act books.

All MLs for the Essex and Herts. division of the **Archdeaconry of Middlesex** are at the **Essex Record Office**, Chelmsford (page 20).

Some Herts. parishes occur in the series of ML abstracts at the **Huntingdon Record Office**.

As the Archdeaconries of St. Albans and Middlesex were in the **Diocese of London** MLs were also issued by the Bishop of London. See under 'London', page 30, for a description of the records, at **Guildhall Library**, and the calendars and indexes to these.

ML records for the **St. Paul's Peculiar** (incl. Albury, Brent and Furneux Pelham) are at **Guildhall Library**, allegations 1686-1841, bonds 1670-1823 (TS index to grooms' names only).

See also **Faculty Office** and **Vicar General**'s ML records, pages 7 and 8.

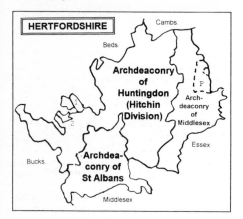

HERTFORDSHIRE

Archdeaconry of Huntingdon (Hitchin Division)

Archdeaconry of Middlesex

Archdeaconry of St Albans

Cambs, Beds, Bucks, Middlesex, Essex, P

Places in the east of Hertfordshire in the jurisdiction of the Archdeaconry of Middlesex Commissary Court of London (Essex and Herts divisions) (diocese of London); and the Peculiar Court of the Dean and Chapter of St. Paul's (**P**):

Albury (**P**); Gt. Amwell; Anstey; Barkway; Barley; Braughing; Brent Pelham (**P**); Broxbourne; Buckland; Cheshunt; Eastwick; Furneux Pelham (**P**); Gilston; Much and Little Hadham; Hoddesden; Gt. and Little Hormead; Hunsdon; Layston; Meesden; Reed; Royston; Sawbridgeworth; Standon; Stanstead Abbots; Stanstead St. Margarets; Stocking Pelham; Bishops Stortford; Thorley; Thundridge; Ware; Widford; Wormley; Wyddial.

Archdeaconry of Bedford (diocese of Lincoln):

Caddington (**1**)   Studham (**2**)

HUNTINGDONSHIRE
(now part of Cambridgeshire)

BTs and MLs for the Archdeaconry of Huntingdon, which was coterminous with the county, are held at the

County Record Office, Huntingdon (a branch of the Cambridgeshire R.O.).

Bishop's Transcripts

Genealogical Sources in Cambridgeshire, Michael Farrar, 2nd edn., 1994, lists all parishes in the county, with covering dates of BTs, indicating gaps of ten or more years. There is also a list of BTs only, available at the **C.R.O.**, Huntingdon. See also the National Index of Parish Registers, **9**, part 1 (1991).

BTs in general start in 1604, to 1627 or 1632, and recommence in 1660 or the 1680s. Even in the C18 there are often large gaps. They end in 1858.

Some parishes have been collated with parish register transcripts. Some parishes have been microfilmed by the Mormons. This film is available at **C.R.O., Cambridge.**

Marriage Licences

Some early allegations, 1610-1614, are listed in British Record Society **42**, pages 219-222.

The main series of bonds and allegations run from 1663 to 1883. Card index at **C.R.O.**, Huntingdon. It has been filmed by the Mormons and film is available at **C.R.O., Cambridge.**

The series includes some Hertfordshire parishes.

At the **Society of Genealogists** there is a MS full alphabetical abstract (chronological within initial) to **Archdeaconry of Huntingdon, Hitchin Registry** act books MLs 1610-1649, and 1714 - but appears to be mainly for 1616-17, 1631-35, 1638-39, 1641. See also the Herts. Genealogist and Antiquary, 2, pp. 41, 141, 149, 208.

See also **Faculty Office** and **Vicar General**'s ML records, pages 7 and 8.

Note. Although there were a few peculiars in the county, they do not appear to have generated any BT or ML records, so no map of ecclesiastical jurisdictions is necessary.

KENT

The county comprised the two Dioceses of Canterbury (East Kent) and Rochester (West Kent). A number of parishes in the latter were in the Peculiar Deanery of Shoreham.

Bishop's Transcripts

All parishes in Kent are listed in the *National Index of Parish Registers* **4** (1980). Exact coverage and gaps are given for the Diocese of Rochester and parishes in the Peculiar Deanery of Shoreham; but starting dates only for the Diocese of Canterbury.

BTs for the Diocese of Canterbury are in the

Cathedral Archives, Canterbury.

Detailed guide to BTs now available. In general they run from *c.*1561 (some from 1558) to 1639 and 1661 to *c.*1900. To 1812 there are two sets for most parishes, the **Archdeaconry** set from C16 (returned Michaelmas to Michaelmas) and the **Consistory** set from 1603 (Lady Day to Lady Day). For 52 exempt parishes there are single sets only.

Returns are also held for Croydon deanery parishes from 1875, burial grounds and some workhouses for the C19.

BTs for 208 parishes for 1640-42 (and a few 1571-7) are at the **House of Lords Record Office,** London. These are shown in the *National Index* **4**. They have also been listed: in the Historical MSS Commission, 4th Report; in *Manuscripts of the House of Lords*, XI; and in the *Genealogists' Magazine* **11**, 10 (June 1953). Modern copies at the **Institute of Heraldic and Genealogical Studies,** *Canterbury*.

Some of the 1640-42 BTs, for 54 parishes, strayed from the House of Lords and at some time were in the possession of J.S. Burn; now acquired by the *Centre for Kentish Studies, Maidstone*.

BTs for the **Diocese of Rochester** are at the *Centre for Kentish Studies (formerly Kent Archives or Record Office), Maidstone*.
In general they start in the early C18.

However, pre-1813 BTs for the parishes in the **Peculiar of the Deanery of Shoreham** are at *Lambeth Palace Library, London*.
These parishes are:listed below.

In general there are a few BTs for the Shoreham Deanery from 1670 to 1712 at the latest, but the remainder for the C18 are missing entirely (except 1743-4 for five parishes, and 1753 for Grayne) until 1799 when they recommence. After 1812 BTs are mainly at the Kent R.O.

Peculiar Deanery of Shoreham (S): Bexley **3**; Brasted; Chevening; Chiddingstone; St. Mary Cray; Crayford **3**; Darenth **4**; Downe **6**; Eynsford; East Farleigh **10**; Farningham; Gillingham **7**; Grain **2**; Halstead; Hayes; Hever; Hunton **10**; Ide Hill; Ifield; Ightham; Keston **6**; Knockholt; Lidsing; East Malling **8**; Meopham; Northfleet **5**; Orpington; Otford; East Peckham **9**; Penshurst; Plaxtol; Sevenoaks; Shoreham; Stanstead; Sundridge; Wrotham.

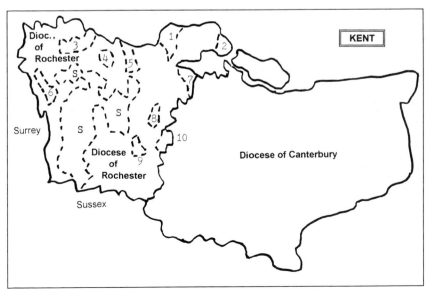

25

Marriage Licences

For the Diocese of Canterbury full abstracts have been published for the complete period 1568-1837: **1568-69, 1574-1646, 1660-1750** (six vols.), by J.M. Cowper (some errors).

1570 (appendix in General Licences, from act book, by A.J.Willis).

1751-1837 (three vols., MLs from act books, bonds and allegations); printed index to whole period. Also TS volumes of General Licences, 1660-1714, which include some additional MLs.

Original records are at **Canterbury Cathedral Archives**. Allegations continue to 1882 and registered licences to 1937.

For the **Diocese of Rochester**, the **Centre for Kentish Studies** (Kent A.O.), Maidstone, has an incomplete series of bonds and allegations for 1637-1639, 1715-16, 1731-67, 1770-72, 1775, 1777-1859, 1877-1949, 1953-86. Chronological MS index includes missing 1799-1840. Microfiche of index published by Kent F.H.S.

MLs for the **Peculiar of the Deanery of Shoreham** are at **Lambeth Palace Library**. A full abstract chronological calendar and index have been prepared, August 1684 - March 1859. At present this is MS (and not available for public consultation) but it is to be typed.

The **Society of Genealogists** has a TS of MLs for Deptford St. Paul, 1776-1835, copied from a private collection of original MLs assembled around 1880.

See also **Faculty Office** and **Vicar General**'s ML records, pages 7 and 8.

LANCASHIRE

(now split between the counties of Lancashire, Greater Manchester and Merseyside; Furness now in Cumbria and southern border area in Cheshire)

Bishop's Transcripts

Lancashire Record Office, Preston

has BTs for virtually all the county, except the Furness area. See *Finding Folk* (1st ed., 1995; 2nd ed. in preparation) for a list of all parishes with starting and finishing dates of BTs (gaps not shown). Some from as early as 1570s, others later C17 or even C19.

BTs for the Furness area, now in Cumbria, are now at **Cumbria R.O.**, *Barrow-in-Furness*, but microfilm copies are available at Preston. See *Cumbrian Ancestors* (Cumbria Archive Service, 2nd edn. 1993).

The only other record offices with BTs for places in Lancashire are:

Borthwick Institute, *York* (page 49): Aughton, Bailey and Chaigley, including Stonyhurst and Hurst Green, in Mitton.

Cumbria R.O., *Kendal* (page 46): Dalton-in-Kendal, in Burton-in-Kendal.

Leeds District Archives (page 49): Ireby (part of Thornton-in-Lonsdale).

Cheshire Record Office (page 13): Latchford (partly in Grappenhall); Mossley (partly in Mottram-in-Longendale); Stalybridge (partly in Mottram-in-Longendale and Stockport); Stockport (partly Lancs.)

Marriage Licences

Lancashire was split between two ecclesiastical jurisdictions, the **Diocese of Chester** (Archdeaconry of Chester), and the **Archdeaconry of Richmond**, respectively south and north of the River Ribble.

Abstracts and indexes for **the Diocese of Chester, 1606-1719**, have been published by the Lancashire and Cheshire Record Society:
from act books, 1606-31, 1639-44, 1661-1700 (vols. 53, 56, 57, 61, 65, 69, 73, 77; additional bonds and allegations may exist 1661-68, 1670-1700);
from bonds and allegations, 1700-1719 (vols. 82, 85, 97, 101).

Abstracts 1719-1723 have been prepared for eventual publication.

Abstracts for 1825 (Jan.-July) for the West Derby area are published in *Liverpool and District Family Historian*, 11, 3-4 (Sept. 1989), and continuing.

Lancashire: MLs continued

The original bonds and allegations are at the

Cheshire Record Office, Chester.

From 1661 onwards the original bonds and allegations are arranged in chronological order. For 1716-1833 they are in alphabetical order by groom, annually. From 1834 to 1858 they are chronological. Rearrangement in alphabetical order by groom, annually, is currently in progress.

Abstracts and indexes for the **Archdeaconry of Richmond, 1648-1755,** have been published by the Lancashire and Cheshire Record Society (vols. 74, 75, 80, 81, 83, 100, 115). The original bonds and allegations are at the *Lancashire Record Office,* 1615, 1633-34, 1636, 1642, 1648-1854, 1861.

MLs for the Diocese of Liverpool, 1880-1907, are also preserved at the *Lancashire Record Office.*

Broughton, Kirkby Ireleth and Seathwaite were in the Peculiar of the Dean and Chapter of York, records at the Borthwick Institute, York, page 49.

See also ML records of the **Archbishop of York,** page 00, and of the **Faculty Office,** page 7.

A typed index of marriages of Lancashire people which took place outside the county, compiled by R. Trunkfield, is available at the *Lancashire Record Office.*

Peculiar of the Dean and Chapter of York (1): Broughton, Kirkby Ireleth, Seathwaite.

Manor of Halton (2):

Diocese of York (3): Aighton, Bailey, Chaigley.

There is an index to **Colne** wills, **1545-1830,** at *Colne Library.*

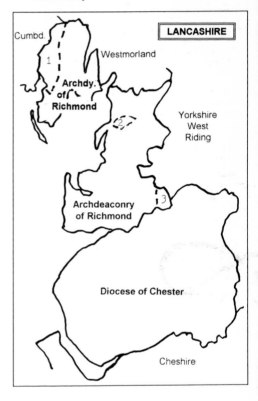

LEICESTERSHIRE

Leicestershire Record Office, Wigston Magna has BTs and MLs for the **Archdeaconry of Leicester** which was coterminous with the county.

Bishop's Transcripts

These are fully listed with all surviving years in the *National Index of Parish Registers*, **6**, Part 3 (1995), which gives dates and location of surviving BTs for all parishes; and in *Handlist of Leicestershire Bishop's Transcripts*, revised by Margaret Smith (Leicester Museums, 1987), £2.50.

In general BTs run regularly from the early C17, but nearly all parishes have several single years surviving from the C16, some as early as the 1560s. They are arranged by parish.

A few BTs for parishes in the **Peculiar of Groby** (Anstey, Newtown Linford, Ratby, Swithland) are at the *Birmingham Central Library (Archives Dept.),* but there are photocopies at the *Leicestershire R.O.*

The *Leicestershire Record Office* also has photocopies for all Rutland parishes of BTs at the *Northamptonshire R.O.*, 1701-1812; and also has copies of BTs of Rutland parishes in peculiars at *Lincolnshire A.O.* (see Northamptonshire section, page 35, for details).

Entries in all BTs (baptisms and marriages) have been included in the I.G.I.

BTs for Ravenstone, 1673-1883, Donisthorpe (St. John 1838-61 and Measham, 1662-1861, are at the *Lichfield Record Office*, see page 40.

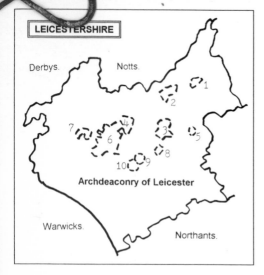

LEICESTERSHIRE

Derbys.   Notts.

7

6

10   9

8

1
2
3
5

Archdeaconry of Leicester

Warwicks.

Northants.

Marriage Licences

Bonds and allegations for the **Archdeaconry of Leicester**, 1570-1891, are at the *Leicestershire Record Office*.

Abstracts, alphabetical by grooms, with abodes of parties and place of marriage, index to brides, **1570-1729**, have been published in British Record Society **38**. The remainder, 1730-1891, are card-indexed at the *Leicestershire Record Office*. They are also in the I.G.I.

ML records for the peculiars, **Leicester St. Margaret**, 1672-1880, **Evington**, 1632-1848, and **Rothley**, 1682-1857, are indexed in B.R.S. **38** (to 1729) and in the *Leics. R.O.* card index thereafter. The few surviving bonds for **Groby** peculiar are with the main Leicester Archdeaconry series.

At the *Society of Genealogists* there are TS calendars of Leics. MLs, 1580-1609 (additional to B.R.S. **38**), Leicester Archdeaconry, 1730-1861, and Leicester St. Margaret Prebend, 1730-1880.

See also **Faculty Office** and **Vicar General**'s ML records, pages 7 and 8.

Places outside the jurisdiction of the archdeaconry of Leicester:

Manor of Rothley:
Barsby **3**; Chadwell **1**; South Croxton **3**; Gaddesby **3**; Grimston **2**; Keyham **8**; Mountsorrel **4**; Rothley **4**; Saxelby **2**; Somerby **5**; Wartnaby **2**; Wycomb **1**.

Peculiar of Groby:
Anstey **6**; Bradgate Park **6**; Charnwood Forest **6**; Cropston **6**; Glenfield **6**; Hallgate **6**; Newton Linford **6**; Ratby **6**; Swanton under Bardon **7**; Swithland **6**.

Manor of Evington - 6

Prebend of St. Margaret, Leicester - 10:
Knighton; Leicester St. Margaret.

LINCOLNSHIRE

Lincolnshire Archives, Lincoln

has BTs and ML records for the whole county. See leaflet *Lincolnshire Archives: Family History.*

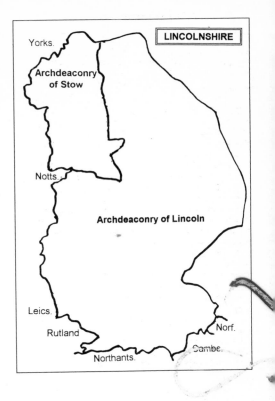

Bishop's Transcripts

These are in two series, the first dating from, at the earliest, 1561 (for the **Archdeaconry of Lincoln**) or 1598 (for the **Archdeaconry of Stow** -- the north-west of the county), to 1812; and the second from 1813 to the end (usually in the 1830s or 1840s). Starting dates for all parishes are given in *A Handlist of the Records of the Bishop of Lincoln and of the Archdeacons of Lincoln and Stow*, Kathleen Major, 1953. A booklet listing BTs is for sale from *Lincolnshire Archives*. Some BTs have been transcribed, in the Foster Library and Brace collections (mainly TS). The BTs have all been microfilmed by the Mormons, so baptisms and marriages should appear in the I.G.I. Access is not normally permitted to the originals, except in cases where the microfilm is illegible.

Marriage Licences

Calendars of the earliest allegation books have been published: 1598, 1606, 1612-1628, in *Lincoln Marriage Licences*, A. Gibbons, 1888. A continuation of this, 1629-36, 1665-70, is in *The Northern Genealogist* **1-6**, and this also includes other early sources. This is arranged alphabetically, but only covers 'A - Harthstone', and was never finished.

However, *Lincolnshire Archives* has modern MS calendars (arranged by year only, not indexed) to all surviving bonds and allegations for the **Archdeaconries of Lincoln** and **Stow** to 1846, and to the **Peculiars of the Dean and Chapter**, 1660-1811 (including Northamptonshire and Rutland peculiars also). There are also contemporary registers of MLs, 1837-1945. The calendars are full abstracts, giving names, abodes, occupations, ages, places of marriage, and date. Originals may be produced in the searchroom for readers to consult. Further indexing work is at present being undertaken with a view to publication.

Bonds for Haxey, 1601-1837, have been published by the Isle of Axholme F.H.S.

See also **Faculty Office** and **Vicar General**'s ML records, pages 7 and 8.

LONDON and MIDDLESEX

The City of London and the county of Middlesex were in the **Diocese of London**.

Bishop's Transcripts

Virtually none survive before 1800; only for the Old Style years 1629-30 and 1639 are they extant in any considerable numbers. Those that do survive are at

Guildhall Library, Aldermanbury, London

and are listed in detail in *Handlist of Parish Registers at Guildhall Library: Part 1: Registers of Church of England parishes within the City of London* (6th ed., 1990); *Part 2: Registers and register transcripts of Church of England Parishes in Greater London outside the City* (7th ed., 1994). See also the *National Index of Parish registers*, *9*, part 5 (1995).

For City of London parishes BTs begin in most cases in 1800 or 1801, and are detailed in Part 1 of the Handlist. In general they rarely need to be consulted as the relevant original registers are, with very few exceptions, also held at *Guildhall Library*.

Guildhall Library also holds registers of Anglican communities overseas, which are similar to BTs in that they are copy registers returned to the Bishops of London and Gibraltar by virtue of their foreign jurisdiction. These are mainly C19 and C20, and are listed in *The British Overseas: A Guide to Records of their Births, Baptisms, Marriages, Deaths and Burials available in the United Kingdom*, 3rd edn., 1994.

There are no BTs amongst the records of the Peculiar of the Dean and Chapter of St. Paul's.

The following parishes were in the **Peculiar Deanery of the Arches**, for which BTs from 1799 or later survive at *Lambeth Palace Library*, London: All Hallows Bread Street, All Hallows Lombard Street, St. Dionis Backchurch, St. Dunstan-in-the-East, St. John the Evangelist Watling Street, St. Leonard Eastcheap, St. Mary Aldermary, St. Mary Bothaw, St. Mary le Bow, St. Michael Crooked Lane, St. Michael Royal, St. Pancras Soper Lane, St. Vedast Foster Lane.

Apart from those at **Guildhall Library**, BTs for the county of Middlesex also date mainly from *c.*1800 or later, the only exception being St. Luke Chelsea (1745-1756). These are mainly at *London Metropolitan Archives (formerly Greater London Record Office), 40 Northampton Road, London EC1R 0HB.*

Marriage Licences

A Guildhall Library leaflet summarises holdings of ML records for London and Middlesex both at that Library and elsewhere. The Diocese of London included, in addition to the City of London, much of Essex and Middlesex, part of Hertfordshire and four Buckinghamshire parishes.

As with the Faculty Office ML records, there are alternative published indexes, C16 and C17. For the relatively few MLs **1520/1-1697**, issued by the 'Vicar General of the Bishop of London', see the full chronological list, with index of names, in Harleian Society **25** (1887).

For **1597-1648** see first British Record Society **62**, and for **1660-1700**, B.R.S. **66**. These are chronological calendars, giving names of parties only, with indexes. Those asterisked are abstracted fully in Harl. Soc. **25** (1597-1610/1) or **26** (1611-1648, 1660/1-C19 - but very few after 1661).

B.R.S. **62** and **66** contain many inaccuracies, and there are copies with MS amendments and references to extant related bonds, by B. Lloyd, in Guildhall Library manuscripts reading room.

From 1700 there are the following indexes or calendars available at the **Guildhall Library** manuscripts searchroom:

1700-1750, TS indexes of both parties (17 vols.);
1751-1826, MS calendars of names of parties, arranged chronologically (6 vols);
1827-1964, MS calendars of names of parties, arranged alphabetically within years, by men's name only (6 vols.).

Amongst the unpublished indexes and calendars held at the Society of Genealogists for C18 are:

1700-1745, TS index (14 vols.);
1700-1780, Great Card Index. The later years may not be completely covered.
1761-1762, TS, by Beric Lloyd.
The original allegations, 1597-9, 1601-48, 1661-1971, 1974-date, are at *Guildhall Library*, but the original books of the Vicar General to 1685, calendared in full for C16 in Harl. Soc. **25**, are at *London Metropolitan Archives*.

Also at *Guildhall Library* are ML records of the:
Archdeacon of London (most of the City; Clerkenwell, Islington and Shoreditch in Middx.), 1666-91 (index by name of both parties);
Dean and Chapter of St. Paul's Cathedral, allegations 1686-1841, bonds 1670-1823 (TS index to grooms' names only). (Jurisdiction: **City**: St. Faith, St. Giles Cripplegate, St. Gregory, St. Helen Bishopgate, and Precinct of Portpool; **Middlesex**: Friern Barnet, Chiswick, West Drayton, Precinct of Hoxton (Shoreditch), St. Luke Old Street, St. Pancras, Stoke Newington, Willesden; also three parishes in Herts. and six in Essex);

Royal Peculiar of St. Katharine by the Tower,

allegations, bonds etc. 1686-89 and 1698-1802 (mainly 1755-1802). 1698 onwards [i.e. Mss 9740-1], MS calendar in Guildhall Library manuscripts reading room, alphabetical by first letter, then chronological (both parties). Printed calendar in alphabetical order in *Home Counties Magazine* 4-6. Also allegations, bonds and licences 1720-1802 [i.e. Ms.9772], not calendared or indexed.

Guildhall Library also holds within parish archives a number of original licences. These are indexed, for the period 1712-1838 only, by names of both parties in Ms. 24657 on the reading room shelves.

ML records for the **Peculiar Deanery of the Arches** are at *Lambeth Palace Library*. These survive from August 1684 to February 1706/7 only. A full abstract calendar has been prepared, with index, but this is not yet available for public consultation.

Harrow with Pinner and Hayes with Norwood were in the Peculiar Deanery of Croydon, whose ML records are also at *Lambeth Palace Library* (see page 43).

MLs for the **Peculiar of the Dean and Chapter of Westminster** are published in (apparently) full, fully abstracted, for the whole period they survive: 1558/9-1646, 1661-1678, 1688-1699, in Harl. Soc. **23** (1886). They are taken from a will register and act books held at the **City of Westminster Archives Centre**, *10 St. Ann's Street, London SW1P 2XR*. They are not licence allegations, only a record of names and parishes plus bonds (1688-99 names only); the licence allegations were apparently destroyed. The Harleian Society volume is an abstract in English of the important data omitting common form clauses in Latin. The places in the Peculiar were the precincts of the Abbey, St. Margaret's Westminster, Paddington, precincts of St. Martin le Grand and parts of the parishes of St. Leonard Foster Lane and St. Anne and St. Agnes; also St. Mary Maldon in Essex.

Also at the **C.W.A.C.** is an account book of fees for MLs issued by the Dean and Chapter, 1772-1804; and an indexed collection of MLs from St. Peter, Eaton Square, 1766-1891.

There is a TS collection, by Crisp, of miscellaneous abstracts of MLs, **1713-1892**, for London and Middlesex. Copies at the *Society of Genealogists* and the *Institute of Historical Research*.

See also **Faculty Office** and **Vicar General**'s ML records, pages 7 and 8. Indexed.

The parishes and chapelries in the city of London and the county of Middlesex are listed below, with the jurisdiction(s) into which they fell indicated as follows:

C: Commissary Court of London (London division); **L**: Archdeaconry of London; **M**: Archdeaconry of Middlesex; **A**: Peculiar Deanery of the Arches; **D**: Peculiar Deanery of Croydon; **P**: Peculiar of the Dean and Chapter of St. Paul's; **K**: Peculiar of St. Katherine-by-the-Tower; **W**: Peculiar of the Dean and Chapter of Westminster; **S**: Archdeaconry Court of Surrey (diocese of Winchester) - parishes in Southwark were still in that county in 1858 (see page 43).

Numbers refer to the map on page 32.

This list is based, for the city, on that in Lewis's *Topographical Dictionary* published in 1831, and includes places that may have been chapelries within other parishes and subsequently became parishes in their own right. Parishes were in the city or in its immediate vicinity unless otherwise stated.

Acton **C3**; St. Alban Wood Street **C**; Allhallows Barking **C**; Allhallows the Great **L**; Allhallows Honey Lane **C**; Allhallows the Less **L;** Allhallows Lombard Street **A**; Allhallows Staining **C**; Allhallows London Wall and St. Augustin Papey **L**; St. Alphage London Wall **L**; St. Andrew Holborn **L13**; St. Andrew Hubbard **C**; St. Andrew Undershaft with St. Mary Axe **C**; St. Andrew-by-the-Wardrobe **L**; St. Anne and St. Agnes Aldersgate with St. John Zachary **W & L**; St. Anne Blackfriars **C**; St. Anne (Soho) Westminster **M**; St. Antholin **C**; Ashford **M19**; St. Augustine Watling Street **L**; Friern Barnet **P2**; St. Bartholomew by the Exchange **L**; St. Bartholomew the Great **L**; St. Bartholomew the Less **L**; Bedfont **M19**; St. Benet Fink **C**; St. Benet Gracechurch **C**; St. Benet Paul's Wharf **C**; St. Benet Sherehog **C**; Bethnal Green, St. Matthew **C1**; St. Botolph Aldersgate **L**; St. Botolph Aldgate **L**; St. Botolph Billingsgate **C**; St. Botolph without Bishopsgate **C**; Bow **C**; Brentford **M19**; St. Bride, Fleet Street **C**; Bromley St. Leonard **C1**; Chelsea **M17**; Chiswick **P16**; Christchurch Greyfriars Newgate Street **L**; Christchurch Southwark **S**; Christchurch Spitalfields **C1**; St. Christopher le Stocks **C**; St. Clement Danes **M**; St. Clement Eastcheap **C**; Cowley **M19**; Cranford **M19**; St. Dionis Backchurch **A**; West Drayton **P9**; St. Dunstan in the East **A**; St. Dunstan in the West **C**; Ealing **C3**; Edgware **C1**; Edmonton **C1**; St. Edmund the King **C**; Enfield **C1**; St. Ethelburga **L**; St. Faith **P**; Feltham **M19**; Finchley **C1**; Fulham **C3**; St. Gabriel Fenchurch **C**; St. George Bloomsbury **C12**; St. George Botolph Lane **C**; St. George in the East **C1**; St. George Hanover Square **M17**; St. George the Martyr and St. Andrew above Bars **L13;** St. George Southwark **S**; St. Giles Cripplegate **P**; St. Giles in the Fields **C12**; St. Gregory by St. Paul's **P**; Greenford **C3**; Hackney **C1**;

London and Middlesex, continued

Monken Hadley or Hadleigh **C1**; Hammersmith **C3**; Hampstead **C1**; Hampton **M19**; Hanwell **M19**; Hanworth **C20**; Harefield **C3**; Harlington **M19**; Harmondsworth **M19**; Harrow **D4**; Hayes **D10**; St. Helen Bishopsgate **P**; Hendon **C1**; Heston **M19**; Highgate **P6**; Hillingdon **M19**; Hornsey **C1**; Hounslow **M19**; Hoxton (Shoreditch) **P**; Ickenham **C3**; Isleworth **M19**; Islington **C1**; St. James Clerkenwell **L13**; St. James Duke's Place **C**; St. James Garlickhythe **C**; St. James (Piccadilly) Westminster **M**; St. John Baptist **L**; St. John Baptist Savoy **L**; St. John Clerkenwell **L13**; St. John Evangelist Watling Street **A**; St. John Evangelist Westminster **W18**; St. John Horsleydown **S**; St. John Millbank (Smith Square) **C**; St. John Zachary **L**; St. Katherine Coleman **L**; St.Katherine Creechurch **C**; St. Katherine by the Tower **K**; Kensington **M17**; Kingsbury **C1**; Laleham **M19**; St. Lawrence Jewry **C**; St. Lawrence Pountney **C**; St. Leonard Eastcheap **A**; St. Leonard Foster **W & C**; St. Leonard Shoreditch **L15**; Limehouse **C1**; Littleton **M19**; St. Luke Old Street **P14**; St. Magnus the Martyr **L**; St. Margaret New Fish Street **C**; St. Margaret Lothbury **L**; St. Margaret Moses **L**; St. Margaret Pattens **C**; St. Margaret Westminster **M & W 18**; St. Martin in the Fields **W & L**; Precincts of St. Martin-le-Grand **W**; St. Martin Ironmonger Lane **C**; St. Martin Ludgate **L**; St. Martin Orgar **C**; St. Martin Outwich **C**; St. Martin Vintry **C**; St. Mary Abchurch **L**; St. Mary Aldermanbury **C**; St. Mary Aldermary **A**; St. Mary-le-bone **C1**; St. Mary Bothaw **A**; St. Mary le Bow **A**; St. Mary Colechurch **L**;

St. Mary at Hill **L**; St. Mary Magdalene Old Fish Street **L;** St. Mary Magdalene Milk Street **C**; St. Mary Mounthaw **L**; St. Mary Somerset **L**: St. Mary Staining **L**; St. Mary le Strand **M**; St. Mary Woolchurch Haw **C**; St. Mary Woolnoth **L**; St. Matthew Friday Street **C**; St. Michael Bassishaw **L**; St. Michael Cornhill **C**; St. Michael Crooked Lane **A**; St. Michael Queenhithe **L**; St. Michael le Quern **L**; St. Michael Royal **A**; St. Michael Wood Street **C**; St. Mildred Bread Street **C**; St. Mildred Poultry **C**; South Mimms **C1**; St. Nicholas Acons **C**; St. Nicholas Cole Abbey **C**; St. Nicholas Olave **C**; Northolt **C3**; Norwood **D10**; St. Olave Hart Street **L**; St. Olave Old Jewry **C**; St. Olave Silver Street **L**; St. Olave Southwark **S**; Paddington **M & W11**; St. Pancras (Middx) **P6**; St. Pancras Soper Lane **A**; St. Paul Covent Garden **M**; St. Peter Cornhill **L**; St. Peter near St. Paul's Wharf **C**; St. Peter le Poer **C**; St. Peter ad Vincula, Tower*; St. Peter Westcheap **L**; Pinner **D4**; Poplar **C1**; Precinct of Portpool **P**; Ruislip **C3**; St. Saviour Southwark **S**; St. Sepulchre **C**; Shadwell St. Paul **C**; Shepperton **M19**; Shoreditch **P**; Staines **M19**; Stanmore **C1**; Stanwell **M19**; St. Stephen Coleman Street **C**; St. Stephen Walbrook **L**; Stepney **C**; Stoke Newington **P7**; Sunbury **M19**; St. Swithin London Stone **C**; Teddington **C20**; St. Thomas the Apostle **L**; Tottenham **C1**; Trinity the Less **L**; Trinity in the Minories **L**; Twickenham **M19**; Uxbridge **M19**; St. Vedast Foster Lane **A**; Wapping St. John **C**; Precincts of Westminster Abbey **W**; Whitechapel **C1**; Willesden **P5**.

*It is not clear into which court's jurisdiction St. Peter ad Vincula fell.

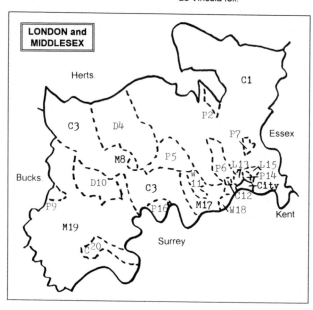

NORFOLK

Norfolk was in the **Diocese of Norwich** and records (except for Emneth, which was in the diocese of Ely) are all at the

Norfolk Record Office, Norwich.

General information on both BTs and MLs is given in *Guide to Genealogical Sources* (N.R.O., 3rd ed., 1993); see also *National Index of Parish Registers 7* (1983), which lists dates of all surviving transcripts.

Bishop's and Archdeacons' Transcripts

Transcripts: In two main series, **Archdeacons'** and **Bishop's**. Before 1812, returns were made to the Archdeacons for six years out of every seven, the seventh normally being a Bishop's Visitation year. From 1813 on all returns were made to the Bishop. Archdeacons' Transcripts are arranged by parish.

Archdeaconry of Norwich: 1600-1610, 1623-1636, 1665-1811 (except Great Yarmouth, 1696-1812, and Castle Rising, 1736-1818).

Archdeaconry of Norfolk: 1725-1811.

The Norwich Archdeaconry was mainly in the north of the county and the Norfolk Archdeaconry in the south, but large areas are exceptions to this.

Bishop's Transcripts, kept in yearly bundles, cover the years 1691, 1698*, 1705, 1708, 1709*, 1713*, 1715, 1716*, 1718*, 1720*, 1721*, 1722, 1723*, 1724, 1728, 1729*, 1730*, 1733, 1734, 1736*, 1739, 1744*, 1746, 1752, 1759, 1762, 1769, 1776, 1783, 1790, 1792*, 1793, 1800, 1802*, 1804*, 1805, 1812, 1813-1933 (1941 for Archdeaconry of Norfolk). Asterisked years are for the Archdeaconry of Norfolk only. Marriages are not included after 1837.

The Archdeacon's Transcripts for most of the 35 Norwich city parishes have been re-sorted into yearly bundles, to facilitate research. The exceptions are the Dean and Chapter parishes.

Transcripts for the **Dean and Chapter Peculiar** cover 1706-1811, and subsequently in the Bishop's series. The parishes in the Peculiar were: the Precincts of the Cathedral, Eaton, Lakenham, St. James and St. Paul, Norwich; Arminghall, West Beckham, Catton, Hindolveston, Martham, Great Plumstead, Sedgeford, Sprowston and Trowse. There are no pre-1813 transcripts for St. Helen's Norwich, or for Great Cressingham.

Marriage Licences

Norwich Consistory Court (for the whole diocese) 1557- 1613 (few); 1628; 1635-1694 (few); 1695-1988. Card index to bonds 1476-1711 (with gaps); lists 1476-1733 (from 1712 incomplete); indexes 1731-1735, 1737-1744, 1749-1751. Incomplete indexes 1712-1733, 1736-1739. Printed index 1563-88 only, *Norwich Consistory Marriage Licences*, W. Rye.

Archdeacon of Norwich: 1590-1609, 1624-1626, 1632-1637, 1660-1681, 1712-1863, 1873-1915.

Bonds 1813-1837 published in *Norfolk Genealogy 23* (1991). Otherwise no index.

Archdeacon of Norfolk: 1541-1602, 1673-1676, 1704, 1706-1711, 1715-1886; also list of lost bonds 1663-1690. Bonds 1813-1837 published in *Norfolk Genealogy 25* (1994).

Dean and Chapter: 1705-1860; list 1725-1750, 1767-1808; list of bonds 1624-1649, 1660-1680 (originals lost) included in list of Norwich Consistory MLs.

Peculiar of Great Cressingham: 1719-1760.

MLs 1624-1860 **for Dean and Chapter and Peculiar of Great Cressingham** published in *Norfolk Genealogy 16* (1984).

At the *Society of Genealogists* there is a 5 vol. TS series of fully alphabetical abstracts, grooms and brides, from the Campling Collection, of Marriages ranging from 1549 to 1799, for Norfolk and Suffolk. These are probably mainly from the Norwich Consistory Court but include many other authorities, some being from the Vicar General and the Faculty Office.

See also **Faculty Office** and **Vicar General**'s ML records, pages 7 and 8.

Parishes in the detached deaneries of Heacham and Burnham (**H**), and Repps and Waxham (**R**), in the archdeaconry of Norfolk and in the detached deaneries of Breccles (**B**) and Thetford (**T**) in the archdeaconry of Norwich; parishes in the peculiars of the Dean and Chapter of Norwich (**DC**), Castle Rising (**CR**), and Great Cressingham (**GC**); and the parish of Emneth in the diocese of Ely (**E**).

Aldborough **R**; Antingham **R**; Arminghall **DC7**; Ashill **B**; Ashmanhaugh **R**; Aylmerton **R**; Bacton **R**; Bagthorpe **H**; Barmer **H**; Barningham Norwood **R**; Barningham Town **R**; East, North and West Barsham, **H**; Barton Turf **R**; Barwick **H**; West Beckham **DC1**; Beeston Regis and St. Lawrence **R**; Bessingham **R**; Gt and Newton Bircham **H**; Bircham Tofts **H**; Bradfield **R**; Brancaster **H**; Breckles **B**; Brumstead **R**; Burnham Deepdale, Norton, Overy, Thorpe, Ulpe and Westgate **H**; Carbrooke **B**; Castle Rising **CR4**; Caston **B**; Catfield **R**; Catton **DC6**;North and South Creake **H**; Gt. Cressingham **GC8**; Cromer **R**; Crostwight **R**; Dilham **R**; Docking **H**; Dunton **H**; Eaton **DC7**; Eccles **R**; Edingthorpe **R**; Little Ellingham **B**; Emneth **E9**; Fakenham **H**; Felbridge **R**; Felmingham **R**; Fring **H**; Fulmodeston cum Croxton **H**; Gatesend **H**; Gimingham **R**; Gresham **R**; Griston **R**; Gunton **R**; Hanworth **R**; Happisburgh **R**; Heacham **H**; Hempstead **R**; Hickling **R**; Hindolveston **DC3**; Holme next the Sea **H**; Honing **R**; Horning **R**; Horsey **R**; Houghton (next Harpley) **H**; Hoveton St. John and St. Peter **R**; Hunstanton **H**; Ingham **R**; Ingoldisthorpe **H**; Irstead **R**; Kettlestone **H**; Knapton **R**; Lakenham **DC7**; Lessingham **R**; Ludham **R**; Martham **DC5**; Matlask **R**; Merton **B**; Metton **R**; Mundesley **R**; Neatishead **R**;

33

Norfolk continued

Northrepps **R**; **Norwich** (Cathedral, St. Helen, St. James, St. Paul) **DC7**; Overstrand **R**; Ovington **B**; Palling **R**; Paston **R**; Plumstead **DC6**; Potter Heigham **R**; Ridlington **R**; Ringstead **H**; Roughton **R**; Roydon near Lynn **CR4**; East and West Rudham **H**; Runton **R**; East Ruston **R**; Little Ryburgh **H**; Saham Toney **B**; Sco Ruston **R**; Scoulton **B**; Sculthorpe **H**; Sedgeford **DC2**; Sheringham **R**; Shernborne **H**; Sidestrand **R**; Sloley **R**; Smallburgh **R**; Snettisham **H**; Little Snoring **H**; Southrepps **R**;

Sprowston **DC6**; Stalham **R**; Stanhoe **H**; Stibbard **H**; Stow Bedon **B**; Suffield **R**; Sustead **R**; Sutton **R**; Swafield **R**; Syderstone **H**; Tatterford **H**; Tattersett **H**; Thetford **T**; Thompson **B**; Thornham **H**; Thorpe Market **R**; Threxton **B**; Thurgarton **R**; Titchwell **H**; Tottington **B**; Triningham **R**; Trowse Newton **DC7**; Trunch **R**; Tunstead **R**; Walcott **R**; North Walsham **R**; Waterden **H**; Watton **B**; Waxham **R**; Westwick **R**; Witton (near North Walsham) **R**; North and South Wootton **CR4**; Worstead **R**.

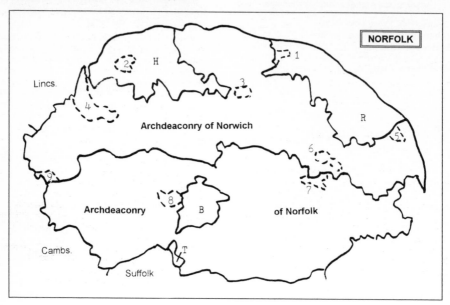

NORTHAMPTONSHIRE and RUTLAND

(Soke of Peterborough now in Cambridgeshire;
Rutland now in Leicestershire)

Northamptonshire Record Office, Northampton

has BTs and MLs for the Diocese of Peterborough,
which covered the whole of the two counties except
for peculiars.

Bishop's Transcripts

These are described in the *National Index of
Parish Registers*, 9, Part 2 (1991), which gives
dates and location of surviving BTs for all parishes.

In general these date from around 1706, with a
few of 1701, and with many gaps. Most BTs at the
Northamptonshire Record Office have been
photocopied to 1812, and gaps photocopied from
original registers when these are already deposited.
The photocopies have been bound into a series of
volumes, by parish, and are on open shelves in the
search room. Those from 1813 on are seen in the
original records.

There are also photocopies at **Leicestershire
Record Office** of BTs of all Rutland parishes held
at Northamptonshire R.O.

There is a typed list of all parishes and extant
years at the **Northamptonshire Record Office**.
Parishes in the Soke of Peterborough, now in
Cambridgeshire, are listed in *Genealogical Sources
in Cambridgeshire*, Cambs. R.O., 2nd edn., 1994,
with starting and finishing dates of BTs, gaps of ten
years or more being shown.

Marriages to 1812 from these BTs originally
formed the basis of a marriage index compiled by
Mr C. Bollen Blore (163 Billing Road, Northampton
NN1 5RS), though this is now mainly from original
registers, and covers two thirds of the county
including all large population centres. Minimum fee
£2 and s.a.e.

BTs of Northamptonshire and Rutland peculiars
are at the

Lincolnshire Archives Office, Lincoln.

Northamptonshire: Apethorpe, Duddington, Gretton,
Nassington, King's Sutton, Wood Newton, Yarwell.
Rutland: Caldecott, Empingham, Ketton, Liddington,
Tixover (copies of these Rutland BTs are at
Leicestershire Record Office).

For Northamptonshire parishes there are
occasional early C17 returns, and no more until
early or mid-C18 (King's Sutton 1605-19 only). For
Rutland, Empingham has late C17 returns also, and
Caldecott are mainly missing C18.

BTs for King's Sutton (Nhants.) 1676-1813 and
also for Banbury (Oxon.), whose hamlet Grimsbury
was in N'hants., both in the Peculiar of Banbury, are
at *Oxfordshire Archives*.

Marriage Licences

There are registers of MLs 1598-1651, 1660-
1665, 1668-1684 (in a confusing overlapping series
for Consistory and Archdeaconry Courts) with a
partial MS abstract by H.I. Longden (H.I.L. vol. 25)
and also a partial card index. Record office staff will
advise on just what is indexed and what is not.

Original bonds survive for 1669-70 and from
January 1679/80, with some C17 years in poor
condition or partly missing. From 1684 bonds have
been flattened and arranged alphabetically by
groom's surname, one bundle per year. Affidavits
survive only from 1823, and these and the bonds
continue into the C20.

There is a card index to bonds in preparation, at
present covering the years 1685-1742. There are
also contemporary calendars to ML bonds, 1729-
1730, 1733/4-46; July 1850 - Jan. 1858.

Peculiar of Banbury (Oxon), **7**
Kings Sutton (Northants); Grimsbury (Northants)
(parish of Banbury)

Peculiar of Empingham (Rutland), **1**
Empingham, Hardwick

Peculiar of Gretton (Northants)
Duddington (**3**), Gretton (**5**)

Peculiar of Ketton (Rutland), **2**
Ketton, Geeston, Tixover

Peculiar of Liddington (Rutland), **4**
Liddington; Caldecott; Thorpe by Water (parish of
Seaton).

Peculiar of Nassington (Northants), **6**
Nassington, Apethorpe, Woodnewton, Yarwell.

Northamptonshire: MLs continued

Places in peculiars are not included in these records. King's Sutton and Grimsbury (Banbury) are included in the TS abstracts and indexes to Oxfordshire peculiars (to 1736) (originals at *Oxfordshire Archives*, indexes at *Oxon. Archives* and *Society of Genealogists*); and (post-1736) with Buckingham Archdeaconry bonds (originals at *Buckinghamshire Record Office*, indexes at *Bucks R.O.*, *Oxon. Archives* and *Bodleian*).

For other peculiars, records at *Lincolnshire Archives Office*, see page 29.

See also **Faculty Office** and **Vicar General**'s ML records, pages 7 and 8.

NORTHUMBERLAND

See with Durham, page 19.

NOTTINGHAMSHIRE

Nottinghamshire formed an Archdeaconry in the Diocese of York, but records of the **Archdeaconry**, and for the large **Peculiar of Southwell**, have long been separated from the main diocesan collection at York. See the *National Index of Parish Registers* 6, Part 2 (1988) for details of BTs for all parishes (including dates of all surviving BTs) and ML records.

Bishop's Transcripts

Original BTs for the whole county are at *Southwell Minster Library, Southwell.*
However, they are also available, on microfilm, at the

Nottinghamshire Archives Office, Nottingham.

They extend from *c.*1600 to *c.*1850, but with many gaps in different parishes. Baptisms probably included in I.G.I.

Peculiar of Southwell BTs 1614–41 were published in Thoroton Society Record Series 1.

Marriage Licences

The original records, for **the Archdeaconry of Nottingham**, are at the

Department of Manuscripts and Special Collections, Hallward Library, University Library, Nottingham

and for **Southwell Peculiar** are at the *Southwell Minster Library*.

Archdeaconry:
Chronological calendar, indexed:
1577, 1590-1648/9, 1653, 1660-1700 (published, British Record Society **58**);

Nottinghamshire: MLs continued

1701-1753 (published, B.R.S. **60**);
1754-1770 (published, Thoroton Society Record Series **10**); (also, list only, 1754-1780, Thoroton Society **10** (Pt. 1), 1942).
Chronological calendar, unindexed:
1771-1780, MS, Nottinghamshire A.O.
1781-1787, TS index, University MSS Dept.
1791-1800, indexed bonds, published (£15 from MSS Dept., University of Nottingham) (1771-80, 1781-90, 1801-10 in preparation).

Southwell Peculiar:
Published chronological calendar, indexed:
1588-1595, 1660-1694, 1700-1754, B.R.S. **58**.
1755-1853, B.R.S. **60**.

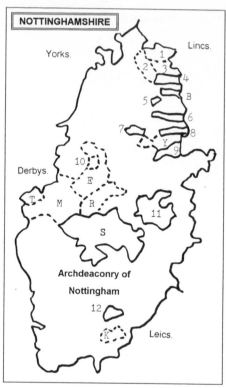

Peculiar of Southwell; Parishes within the area marked 'S' unless are they are numbered.

Beckingham **4**; Bleasby; Blidworth; Calverton; Carlton on Trent **11**; Caunton **11**; Cropwell Bishop **12**; Darlton **9**; Dunham **9**; Eaton **7**; Edingley; Farnsfield; Halam; Halloughton; Holme **11**; Kirklington; North Leverton **6**; Morton; Ragnall **9**; Rampton **8**; Southwell; Upton; South Wheatley **5**; Woodborough.

Nottinghamshire: MLs continued

For the **Peculiar of the Vicar of Kinoulton** there is an MS transcript of allegations, 1740-1823, in E. Young, 'Gleanings from Parish Chests' (Cambs.), pp. 182-87, at the *Society of Genealogists*.

The Nottinghamshire parishes of Askham, East Drayton, Laneham, Misterton, Stokeham, and West Stockwith were in the **Peculiar of the Dean and Chapter of York**, for details see pages 49-50.

As Nottinghamshire was in the Diocese and Province of York, MLs were also issued by the **Archbishop's Court**, see page 49: and see also the **Faculty Office** ML records, page 7.

OXFORDSHIRE

Oxfordshire was in the Diocese of Oxford. Nearly all BTs and ML records are at the county record office, *Oxfordshire Archives, Oxford.*

Bishop's Transcripts

The regular series date from about 1720, but there are usually several in the 1680s. For parishes in peculiars, round Banbury, Dorchester and Thame, there are a few early C17 and a regular series from 1660s. Full details of covering dates and major gaps are in *Oxfordshire Parish Registers and Bishop' Transcripts*, C.G. Harris, Oxon. F.H.S., 5th edn., 1997. This supersedes the *National Index of Parish Registers* **5** (1966).

There are microfilms of parishes A-F at the *Society of Genealogists*.

Buckinghamshire Record Office holds BTs for Newington (Peculiar of Monks Risborough), 1604-1723, 1736-1828; Caversfield (formerly Bucks.), 1807, 1813-41, 1843-46; Horley (Peculiar of Banbury), 1813, 1824-28, 1831-32, 1838-41; and Hornton (Peculiar of Banbury) 1813, 1824-28, 1831-32, 1838-39, 1841.

Marriage Licences

There are 4 series of ML bonds and allegations:

Oxford Diocesan bonds and allegations, 1661-1850. A very good TS alphabetical abstract with full details and index to brides. Copies at *Oxfordshire Archives* and the *Society of Genealogists*.

Oxford Archdeacon's bonds and allegations, 1634-36, 1664-1856. Photostat of MS index to grooms only, alphabetical within each year, to 1849 only; also, fully alphabetical TS index to this, but continuing to 1856. Copies of both indexes at *Oxfordshire Archives* and *Society of Genealogists*.

Oxfordshire, Berkshire and Buckinghamshire Peculiars bonds, mainly later C17 to 1736, but some bonds back to 1623, and Dorchester peculiar continuing to 1836, Langford to 1814. Fully alphabetical TS abstract, index to brides, at *Oxfordshire Archives* and *Society of Genealogists*.

Oxfordshire: MLs continued

Buckingham Archdeaconry bonds, late C17 to mid-C19. A good TS alphabetical abstract, index to brides. Includes post-1736 bonds for Oxfordshire peculiars of Thame, Great Milton, Banbury, Cropredy, Horley and Hornton. Copies at *Oxfordshire Archives, Bodleian (Dept. of Western MSS)* and *Buckinghamshire R.O.* (origs. at *Bucks R.O.*). See *Oxon. Family Historian*, 1,9 (Autumn 1979).

See also **Faculty Office** and **Vicar General**'s ML records, pages 7 and 8.

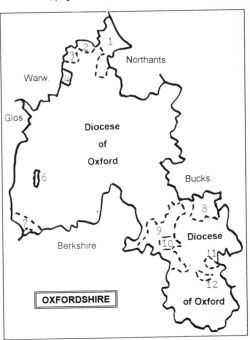

Places in Oxfordshire outside the jurisdiction of the consistory and archdeaconry courts of Oxford:

B : Peculiar of Banbury and Cropredy
M : Peculiar of Monks Risborough

Banbury **B1**; Benson (Bensington) **9**; Britwell Prior **9**; Chiselhampton **9**; Clifton Hampden **9**; Claydon **B1**; Cropredy **B1**; Dorchester **9**; Drayton St. Leonard **9**; Horley **B2**; Hornton **B2**; Langford **7**; Marsh Baldon **9**; Gt. Milton **9**; Mollington **B1**; Nettlebed **12**; Newington **M10**; Pishill **11**; Shenington (Glos., see page 21) **3**; Sibford (parish of Swalcliffe) **4**; Stadhampton **9**; Sydenham **8**; Tetsworth **8**; Thame **8**; Toot Baldon **9**; Warborough **9**; Wardington **B1**; Widford (Glos.) **6**.

RUTLAND

See with Northamptonshire, pages 35 and 36.

SHROPSHIRE

The county was mainly divided between two dioceses, Lichfield (the north and east), and Hereford (the south and west). A few extreme north-western parishes were in the Diocese of St. Asaph. The *National Index of Parish Registers* **5** (1966) lists all parishes and shows in which jurisdiction they lay.

Bishop's Transcripts

Records for the Diocese of Lichfield are at the

Lichfield Record Office.

For details, see under 'Staffordshire and Derbyshire', page 40. Covering dates and major gaps are given in the *National Index* **5**.

BTs for the Shropshire parishes in the **Diocese of St. Asaph** are also at Lichfield: Kinnerley, Knockin, Llanyblodwel, Llanmynech, Melverley, Oswestry St. Martin, Selattyn and Whittington.

Records for the **Diocese of Hereford** are at the *Hereford Record Office*, page 23.

BTs for Alveley, Bridgnorth, Claverley and Quatford, 1636-1812, in the **Peculiar of Bridgnorth**, are at the *British Library (Manuscript Collections), London* [Add. MSS. 28736-7, 28739-40].

Places in Shropshire outside the jurisdictions of the consistory courts of Lichfield and Hereford.

Diocese of St. Asaph
Kinnerley, Knockin, Llanyblodwel, Llanmynech, Melverley, Oswestry, St. Martins, Selattyn, Whittington.

Royal Free Chapel of Shrewsbury St. Mary
Albrighton (**5**); Astley (**6**); Clive (**4**); Shrewsbury St. Mary (**7**)

Peculiar of Longdon on Tern (8)

Peculiar of Wombridge Abbey (9)

Peculiar of Ashford Carbonell (12)

Peculiar Deanery of Bridgnorth
Bridgnorth (**10**); Alveley (**11**); Bobbington (**11**); Claverley (**11**); Quatford (**10**).

Manor of Ellesmere (1)
Ellesmere, Colemeare, Lyneal, Welshampton

Peculiar of Prees
Calverhall (**3**); Darliston (**3**); Prees (**3**); Whixall (**2**)

Diocese of Worcester
Halesowen (Salop, detached).

Marriage Licences

Like the BTs, for the dioceses of Lichfield and Hereford these are in the appropriate diocesan record offices, and are described on the same pages.

Also at Lichfield are the bonds and allegations for the Shropshire peculiars of Longdon upon Tern, 1837, 1843; Wombridge, 1787-1821; Prees (Calverhall, Whixall), 1671-1864; and St. Mary, Shrewsbury, 1835, 1856-88.

Earlier bonds and allegations for the **Peculiar of St. Mary, Shrewsbury**, 1663-1842, are at *Shropshire Records and Research Centre, Shrewsbury* (see *Shropshire F.H.S. Journal*, **5**, 2, June 1984).

Bonds and allegations for the Shropshire parishes in the **Diocese of St. Asaph** (listed above), from 1690 on, are at the *National Library of Wales, Aberystwyth*, page 53.

For the **Peculiar of Wombridge** there is a TS of bonds, 1787-1821, by D.A. Grant, at *Lichfield Record Office* and the *Society of Genealogists*.

See also **Faculty Office** and **Vicar General**'s ML records, pages 7 and 8.

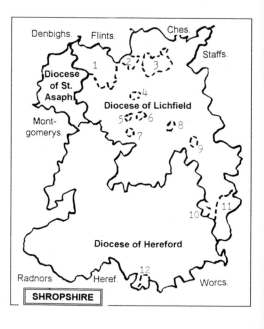

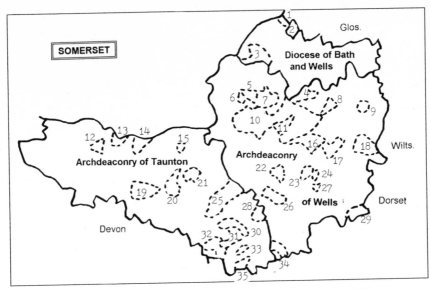

Somerset parishes outside archdeaconry jurisdiction:

B: Consistory court of Bristol,
C: Consistory court of the Dean and Chapter of Wells;
D: Consistory court of the Dean of Wells;
I: Royal peculiar court of Ilminster;
P: other Wells peculiar and prebendal courts.

Abbots Leigh **B2**; (Chapel) Allerton **D10**; Ashill **P30**; South Barrow **C27**; Biddisham **D6**; Binegar **D8**; Bishops Lydeard **C20**; Broomfield **D21**; Buckland Dinham **P9**; Carhampton **D13**; Cheddar **C7**; Chesterblade **D17**; Chilcompton **D8**; Combe St. Nicholas **C32**; Compton Bishop **P5**; Compton Dundon **P22**; Cudworth **P33**; North Curry **C25**; St. Decumans **P14**; Dinder **D10**; Easton in Gordano **P1**; Evercreech **D17**; Fitzhead (pec. of Wiveliscombe) **P19**; East Harptree **P4**; Haselbury Plucknett **P34**; West Hatch **C25**; Henstridge **P29**; Ilminster **I-31**; Ilton **P30**; Kenn (pec. of Yatton) **P3**; Kingsbury Episcopi **P28**; Knowle (pec. of Cudworth) **P33**; East Lambrook (pec. of Kingsbury) **P28**; Litton **P4**; Lovington **C24**; Bishops Lydeard C20; West Lydford **P23**; Mark **D10**; Pilton **P16**; Priddy **D10**; St. Decumans **P14**; Stoke St. Gregory **C25**; Nether Stowey **D15**; Long Sutton **C26**; Timberscombe **P12**; Wedmore **D10**; Wells (St. Cuthbert) **D10**; (Liberty of St. Andrews) **C10**; Westbury **D10**; Whitelackington **P30**; Winsham **C36**; Witham Friary **P18**; Wiveliscombe **P19**; Wookey **P11**; North Wootton **P16**; Yatton **P3**.

SOMERSET

Somerset Record Office, Taunton

has BTs and MLs for virtually all the county, which comprised the **Diocese of Bath and Wells**.

Bishop's Transcripts

These start c.1598, with the usual partial coverage of C17 and poorer than usual coverage of C18, good from 1800 on. They are arranged by parish, each parish having three bundles, to 1812, 1813-1837, post-1837. There is a card index of parishes showing surviving years. About one third are available in MS indexed transcripts by E. Dwelly.

BTs for Abbots Leigh, Bedminster and Brislington are at the *Bristol Record Office*, page 21.

Marriage Licences

These date from 1574 (few before 1645) to 1899, for the whole diocese and county. Col. H.R. Phipps' abstracts of Bath and Wells diocesan records includes MLs 1583-1676 from licence books (MS at *Somerset Record Office*). Surname Index, 1583-1681, by Adrian J. Webb, published 1995, £9.00, by Harry Galloway Publishing, The Cottage, Manor Terrace, Paignton, Devon TQ3 3RQ. Phipps' abstracts and Webb's index available on microfiche (set of 30), £25.00 from Harry Galloway Publishing. For **1645-1755** full indexed abstracts have been published in *Marriage Allegation Bonds of the Bishops of Bath and Wells*, A.J. Jewers, but this has been found to be incomplete. However, it has been republished on microfiche, with 'Amendments... 1672-76' and index of occupations, 9 fiche, £11.95 from Harry Galloway Publishing.

Original bonds and allegations are in annual bundles, arranged alphabetically. Card index in searchroom, 1756-1805. Indexing of bonds and allegations for places outside diocesan or archdeaconry jurisdiction, c.1750 on, in progress.

The *Society of Genealogists* has TS indexes to ML records, 1606-07, 1618-21, 1624-37, 1640-41, 1663-65, 1672-76.

Abbots Leigh (Bristol Diocese), see page 22.

See also **Faculty Office** and **Vicar General**'s ML records, pages 7 and 8.

STAFFORDSHIRE and DERBYSHIRE
(the southern tip of Staffordshire, round Walsall, Wednesbury, West Bromwich and Wolverhampton, is now in the county of West Midlands)

These two counties were both entirely within the Diocese of Lichfield, whose records are now at the

Lichfield Record Office, Lichfield.

There is a published Guide: *Staffordshire Record Office Cumulative Handlist, Part I, Lichfield Joint Record Office: Diocesan, Probate and Church Commissioners' Records* (Staffs. C.C., 1970), which describes BTs and ML records briefly.

Bishop's Transcripts

These usually begin in the 1660s, though there are very occasional C16 survivals and a few pre-Commonwealth C17. In general they are fairly complete from 1700, and for many parishes from c.1660. Incumbents in the 1690s seem to have been encouraged to fill up post-1660 gaps.

They are arranged in two series, to 1812, and from 1813 on. All Staffordshire parishes are listed in the *National Index of Parish Registers* **6**, part 1 (1982), showing covering years and gaps; and Derbyshire parishes are in **the National Index of Parish Registers, 6**, part 5 (1995).

Marriage Licences

Bonds and allegations are in a single chronological series, with a small bundle for the period pre-1660, and yearly bundles thereafter. Within years they are sorted by initial letter of the groom's name, but no further.

Indexes: (1) MS, to all bonds to 1700. This is in fact a calendar, chronological within initial letter of groom's name, giving names of each party and place.

(2) **1700-1704** (MS, compiled 1878), fully alphabetical for each year, surnames only, but giving abodes, place of marriage, and exact date.

(3) **1700-1710** (MS). Calendar, year by year, giving surnames only.

(4) **1711, 1712, 1713**. TS for each year, full abstract, arranged alphabetically by grooms, with index to brides.

(5) **1711-16**. B.M.S.G.H. index on fiche, 1714-16 arranged undergroom's name by initial letter (not alphabetical within letter); indexed, bride and groom.

No indexes after 1716.

There are separate series of ML records for peculiars (mostly indexed by Mrs D. Grant, 115 Clayton Road, Newcastle, Staffs. ST5 3EW, except Dean and Chapter and Dean of Lichfield. Searches undertaken in return for s.a.e. and donation; TS copies at *Lichfield Record Office* and the *Society of Genealogists*):

Dean and Chapter of Lichfield (*Derbys.*: Ashford, Bakewell, Baslow, Beeley, Buxton, Chapel en le Frith, Chelmorton, Fairfield, Hope, Kniveton, Longston, Monyash, Peak Forest, Sheldon, Taddington, Tideswell, Wormhill; *Staffs.*: Cannock, Farewell, Harborne; Lichfield Close; Rugeley, Smethwick): 1624-1890.

Dean of Lichfield (Adbaston, Brewood, Lichfield) 1660-1864;

Alrewas (Kings Bromley, Edingale, Mavesyn and Pipe Ridware) 1628-45, 1660-1855; also at *Staffordshire Record Office*, 1573, 1585 and 1822-3, Ts at *Lichfield Record Office*;

Colwich (Fradswell) 1666-1875;

Eccleshall (Broughton, Chapel Chorlton, Cotes Heath, Croxton) 1663-1861;

Gnosall 1666-1866 (TS list to 1776);

Handsacre and Armitage (Hints, Norton) 1663-1838;

Hartington (Earl Sterndale) 1666, 1675-1715, 1754-80, 1788-1867;

High Offley 1666-1700, 1742-1869;

Longdon 1665-1839;

Penkridge (Coppenhall, Dunston, Shareshill, Stretton) 1661-1871;

Stafford St. Chad, Tipton (Peculiar of **Prees**) 1671-1864;

Sawley 1677-1768, 1773-1843;

Tettenhall (Codsall) 1676-89, 1705-1856 (*Staffs. Hist. Collns.*, 1931, pp. 52-57);

Weeford 1660-1855;

Whittington and Baswich (Acton Trussell, Bednall) 1665-1855;

Wolverhampton (Bentley, Bilston, Featherstone, Hatherton, Hilton, Kinvaston, Pelsall, Wednesfield, Willenhall) 1621-1846. TS 1621-1730 by N.W. Tildesley (indexed). 1730/1-1846, published in *Staffs. Hist. Collns.*, 1931 (indexed);

Miscellaneous MLs, mainly Peak District, 1615-1641, 1660-1720 (270), TS, chronological, also at *Society of Genealogists*.

See also **Faculty Office** and **Vicar General**'s ML records, pages 7 and 8.

Staffordshire and Derbyshire, continued

Places in the jurisdiction of courts other than the consistory court of Lichfield. All places in peculiars are likely to appear also in the consistory court records, and some places not actually in peculiars may still nevertheless be found in records of peculiars.

Staffordshire
(places in area '**B**' unless otherwise shown, except Stafford St. Chad). Clent and Dudley were in the diocese of Worcester.

Acton Trussell; Adbaston **7**; Alrewas; Upper Arley **13**; Armitage; Baswich; Bednall; Bentley; Bilbrook; Bilston; Blithbury; Branstone **5**; Brewood; Bromley Regis; Broughton **7**; Brownhills; Burton on Trent **5**; Bushbury; Cannock; Charnes **7**; Chorlton **7**; Clent **14**; Codsall; Colwich; Compton in Tettenhall; Congreve; Coppenhall; Cotes **7**; Drayton in Hales **6**; Dudley (Worcs) **11**; Dunston; Eccleshall **7**; Edingale **9**; Farewell; Fradley; Fradswell **8**; Gnosall **7**; Hammerwich; Handsacre; Harborne **12**; Haselour; Hatherton; Great Haywood; Hilton in Wolverhampton; Hints; Horninglow **5**; Kings Bromley; Kinvaston; Levedale; Lichfield; Longdon, Mavesyn Ridware; Norton Canes; Oaken; High Offley **7**; Ogley Hay; Packington; Pattingham; Pelsall; Penkridge; Perton; Pipe Ridware; Rodbaston; Rugeley; Saredon; Sedgley **10**; Shareshill; Shobnall **5**; Shugborough; Slindon **7**; Smethwick **12**; Stafford St. Chad; Streethay; Stretton in Burton **5**; Stretton in Penkridge; Sugnall **7**; Swinfen; Tettenhall; Tipton; Trescott; Tyrley **6**; Wall; Walton **7**; Water Eaton; Wednesfield; Weeford; The Wergs; Wetmore **5**; Whittington; Willenhall; Wolverhampton; Wrottesley; Wyrley; Yoxall.

Derbyshire
(places in area '**A**' unless otherwise shown).

Ashford; Bakewell; Baslow; Beeley; Biggin; Breaston **3**; Burbage; Buxton; Chapel-en-le-Frith; Chelmorton; Dale Abbey **2**; Long Eaton **3**; Fairfield; Hartington; Hope; Kniveton **1**; Longstone; Monyash; High Needham; Peak Forest; Risley **3**; Sandiacre **3**; Sawley **3**; Sheldon; Stapenhill **4**; Earl Sterndale; Taddington; Tideswell; Wilne; Winshall **3**; Winster; Wormhill.

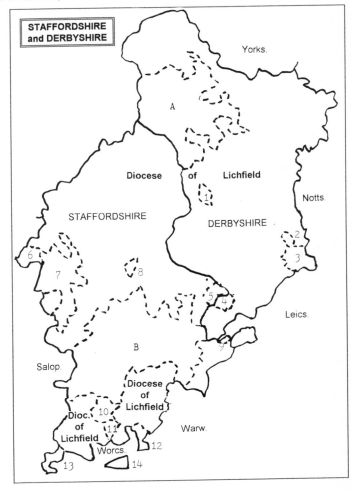

41

SUFFOLK

Until 1974 the county was divided administratively into East Suffolk (Ipswich), ecclesiastically the **Archdeaconry of Suffolk**, and West Suffolk (Bury St. Edmunds), the **Archdeaconry of Sudbury**. Records for the county are split between branches of the *Suffolk Record Office* at *Ipswich, Bury St. Edmunds* and *Lowestoft*.

There are leaflet notes for genealogists, *a Guide to Genealogical Sources* (4th ed., 1993, £6.50) and see also the *National Index of Parish Registers 7* (1983), which lists dates of all surviving transcripts.

'Bishop's' or Archdeacons' Transcripts

As in Norfolk these are in fact Archdeacons' rather than Bishop's Transcripts; or Register Bills.

Whilst the original documents for the **Archdeaconries of Suffolk** and **Sudbury** are respectively at *Ipswich* and *Bury St. Edmunds*, these two branches have microfilm for the whole county (which is always produced for searchers), while the *Lowestoft* branch has microfilms for the Archdeaconry of Suffolk only.

The records are arranged chronologically by archdeaconry, a single sequence for each year, alphabetically by deanery; until 1812 for the Archdeaconry of Suffolk and until 1817 for Sudbury. After these dates one alphabetical sequence for each archdeaconry.

Archdeaconry of Suffolk: dates covered: 1685-1691, 1689/9, 1705/6, 1708/9, 1711-1875.

Archdeaconry of Sudbury: These run from as early as 1563 in some cases, but are often incomplete for many parishes until C18. 1642-1660 and 1685 are missing entirely. A list of extant BTs 1563-1650 is published in *Proceedings of the Suffolk Institute of Archaeology*, XI, pp. 254-266, which also gives a list of years for which there are bundles, 1640-1811. Microfilm coverage ends in 1853, but there are later originals for about a fifth of the parishes, the latest being 1883.

Microfiche copies of original registers and microfilm copies of the extensive collections of modern transcripts at both branches largely supplant reference to the register bills. Their chief value is that they enable a search of an entire archdeaconry or a number of deaneries to be made for a single 'Visitation Year', where the date of the event is known but the place is uncertain. Microfilms of BTs of parishes in Fordham deanery are also held by *Cambs. R.O.*, *Cambridge*.

Exceptions: Freckenham in the **Peculiar of the Bishop of Rochester**, 1673-1813 only (with gaps). Parishes in the **Peculiar of the Archbishop of Canterbury**: Hadleigh, 1795-1803, 1840, 1854-1863 only; Moulton, 1840 only; Monks Eleigh, none; all at *Suffolk Record Office*, Bury St. Edmunds.

Marriage Licences

The county of Suffolk was wholly within in the **Diocese of Norwich** until 1837, so MLs could be issued by the Bishop's Consistory Court, see page 33. See also Campling Collection, below.

Archdeaconry of Suffolk (records at *Suffolk R.O.*, *Ipswich*). There are original bonds for 1663-1678, 1684-1800, 1802-1825, 1828-1859, with indexes, 1663-1750 (ed. F.A. Crisp, privately published 1900); 1751-1825, 1831-1850 (by John Glyde, photocopy of MS). Also registers of licences, 1610-1648, 1663-1664, 1673-1707; indexes, 1613-1674 (ed. F.A. Crisp, privately published 1902); 1675-1707 (by John Glyde, photocopy of MS).

Various Archdeaconry of Suffolk bonds, allegations and indexes, 1613-1900 (with gaps), are available on microfilm at the *Lowestoft* branch.

Archdeaconry of Sudbury: 1683-1839, published calendar and index, Harleian Society **69-72** (somewhat inaccurate, details of bondsmen often omitted). Notes of earlier MLs 1577-93, 1606-11, 1660-66, occurring in administration books *etc.* are card indexed.

Monks Eleigh, Hadleigh and Moulton were in the **Peculiar of the Archbishop of Canterbury in the Peculiar Deanery of Bocking**. Marriage allegations and bonds, 1771-1831, calendared and indexed (TS in preparation) are at *Lambeth Palace Library*.

At the *Society of Genealogists* there is a 5 vol. TS series of fully alphabetical abstracts, grooms and brides, from the Campling Collection, of Marriages ranging from 1549 to 1799, for Norfolk and Suffolk. These are probably mainly from the Norwich Consistory Court, but include many other authorities, some being from the Vicar General and Faculty Office.

See also **Faculty Office** and **Vicar General**'s ML records, pages 7 and 8.

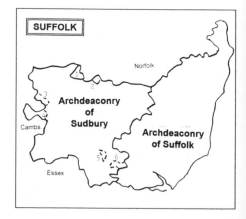

SUFFOLK

Norfolk

Archdeaconry of Sudbury

Archdeaconry of Suffolk

Cambs

Essex

SURREY

(much of Surrey is now in the Greater London area)

See *Guide to Surrey Bishop's Transcripts, Marriage Licences and Probate Records*, West Surrey F.H.S., 1990.

Until 1837 the whole county, apart from the Peculiars, constituted the Archdeaconry of Surrey within the Diocese of Winchester.

Bishop's Transcripts

The *National Index of Parish Registers* **4** (1980) (new ed., Surrey only, 1990) lists all parishes and years of surviving BTs with their location. These are sparse, and few parishes have more than a few pre-1800, most only a year or two. There are BTs for several parishes in the late 1580s, but nothing more until the 1670s, when most parishes have a year or two. For the C18 there are generally none at all, though some parishes have 1717-18 and/or 1729-1730 and a few have a run towards the end of the century. Between 1800 and 1840 most parishes are complete, but often unfit for production.

BTs for all of Surrey except some for the peculiars are at *London Metropolitan Archives (formerly G.L.R.O), 40 Northampton Road, London EC1R 0HB.*

The **Peculiar of the Deanery of Croydon** covered the parishes of Barnes, Burstow, Charlwood, Cheam, Croydon, Horsley East, Merstham, Mortlake, Newington St. Mary, Putney and Wimbledon. Some BTs for these parishes, especially for the period 1799-1813 and earlier, are deposited at *Lambeth Palace Library, London.*

Later BTs are mostly at the Greater London Record Office.

Marriage Licences

For the **Bishop of Winchester's Commissary Court for the Archdeaconry of Surrey** these are at *London Metropolitan Archives*, and date from 1673, but are not complete until 1726. Many are unfit for production. Allegations **1673-1770** were printed by A.R. Bax (1907). This is a chronological calendar giving full details, indexed. Copies are at the *Society of Genealogists* and *Surrey Record Office, Kingston* (until mid-1998; thereafter at *Woking*), but not at *London Metropolitan Archives*.

After 1770, contemporary index only, on microfilm at *London Metropolitan Archives*. Allegations for Aug. 1822 to March 1823 are published in *Root and Branch* **13**, 1 and 2 (1986).

A few MLs occur in *Marriage and Other Licences in the Commissary Court of Surrey*, A.R. Bax (1893) taken from act books, 1662-1665.

There is an index to 'Southwark MLs' 1754-1908 (10,000), various jurisdictions, at the *Minet Library (Lambeth Archives Dept.), 52 Knatchbull Road, London SE5 9QY.*

ML records for the **Peculiar Deanery of Croydon** (parishes listed below) are at *Lambeth Palace Library*. A full abstract calendar has been prepared, with index, for the full period, August 1684 to December 1818, but this is not yet available for public consultation.

It is also worth consulting the ML records of the Bishop of London at *Guildhall Library*, see page 30.

See also **Faculty Office** and **Vicar General**'s ML records, pages 7 and 8.

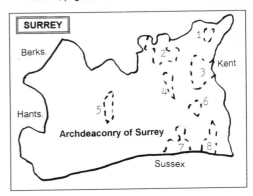

Surrey parishes in the **Peculiar of the Archbishop of Canterbury in the Deanery of Croydon**:

1. Church Newington, Walworth St. Peter.
2. Barnes, Mortlake, Putney, Roehampton, Wimbledon.
3. Croydon.
4. Cheam.
5. East Horsley.
6. Merstham.
7. Charlwood.
8. Burstow

SUSSEX

BTs and MLs for the **Diocese of Chichester**, which was co-terminous with the county of Sussex, are at the

West Sussex Record Office, Chichester.

These are described in the *National Index of Parish Registers* **4** (1980), in the *Genealogists' Guide to the West Sussex Record Office*, Peter M. Wilkinson (1994); and, for East Sussex parishes only, in the *Index of East Sussex Parish Records 1270-1870*, M.J. Burchall (Sussex F.H.G., 1975). All include covering dates of BTs.

43

Bishop's Transcripts

These are arranged by parish and are listed with all surviving years in *A Handlist of the Bishops' Transcripts 1567-1936*, W.S.C.C., 1970; and in the *National Index of Parish Registers* **4**.

The BTs for the **Archdeaconry of Chichester** (West Sussex) extend from 1567 to *c*.1860, with a few continuing into C20; and for **the Archdeaconry of Lewes** (East Sussex) from 1606 (a few from 1592) to 1912.

Peculiars:

Dean of Chichester (most of Chichester, Fishbourne and Rumboldswyke), 1591-1912.

Deanery of Pagham and Tarring (South Bersted, Chichester All Saints, Durrington, Heene, East Lavant, Pagham, Patching, Slindon, Tangmere, West Tarring, Plaistow in Kirdford): 1610-1912.

Deanery of South Malling (Buxted, Edburton, Framfield, Glynde, Hadlow Down, Isfield, Lewes St. Thomas at Cliffe, Lindfield, Mayfield, Ringmer, S. Malling, Stanmer, Uckfield, Wadhurst; E. Chiltington, Hartfield, Withyham, Wivelsfield): 1662-1908.

Deanery of Battle (Battle, Netherfield): 1730-1890.

Few parishes have a complete series to 1641, but for the period 1700 to *c*.1850 a very full series survives for almost all places. There are TS copies of many early BTs at *West Sussex R.O.* There are also parish indexes of baptisms and marriages from BTs and parish registers, prepared by the Mormons, available on microfilm.

West Sussex R.O. also holds microfilm of the complete w.H. Challen collection (mid c20) of Sussex BTs and PRs (from *Guildhall Library, London*). In some cases these include copies of E.H. Dunkin's transcripts of C16 and C17 BTs of which the originals are now lost (see *Sussex Archaeological Society*, below).

Sussex Archaeological Society, *Barbican House, Lewes* has late C19 copies, made by E.H.W. Dunkin, of C16-17 BTs of which the originals are now lost; and TS copies of BTs made by W.H. Challen (see *W.S.R.O.*, above).

Marriage Licences

Registers of MLs together with original bonds and allegations survive from the C16, for the same jurisdictions as for the BTs described above. The majority of pre-1840 MLs have been calendared and indexed:

Chichester Archdeaconry:
1575-1730, 1731-1774, 1775-1800 (Sussex Record Society **12**, **32**, **35**); 1801-1840 (card index).

Lewes Archdeaconry:
1574-83 (British Record Society **24**, p. 447); 1586-1643, 1670-1729 (Sussex R.S. **1**, **6**); 1772-1837 (Sussex R.S. **25**, **26**) (MLs for gaps do not survive).

Peculiars: Dean of Chichester:
1583-1730 (S.R.S. **12**); 1731-1840 (card index).

Deanery of Pagham and Tarring, and **All Saints Chichester:**
1579-1730 (S.R.S. **12**); 1731-1840 (card index).

Deanery of South Malling:
1620-1732 (S.R.S. **6**); 1772-1837 (S.R.S. **25**, **26**). The series of originals continue to the 1940s.

See also **Faculty Office** and **Vicar General**'s ML records, pages 7 and 8.

(Pre-1974) West Sussex parishes in the archdeaconry of Lewes: Beeding, Crawley, Cowfold, Henfield, Kingston, Ifield, Shermanbury, Old and New Shoreham, Southwick, Woodmancote.

Sussex parishes outside the jurisdiction of the archdeaconries of Lewes and Chichester.

Deanery of Battle: Battle, Netherfield, **5**.

Peculiar of the Dean of Chichester: Chichester (all except All SS.), Fishbourne, Rumboldswyke, **7**.

Deanery of South Malling: 3: Buxted, Framfield, Glynde, Isfield, Lewes St Thomas at Cliffe, South Malling, Mayfield, Ringmer, Uckfield, Wadhurst; Edburton **13**; Lindfield **4**; Stanmer **14**.

Deaneries of Pagham and Tarring: Sth Bersted **9**; Chichester All SS **7**, Durrington **12**, Heene **12**, East Lavant **6**, Pagham **9**, Patching **11**, Plaistow in Kirdford **1**, Slindon **10**, Tangmere **8**, W. Tarring **12**.

Diocese of Rochester: Lamberhurst **2**.

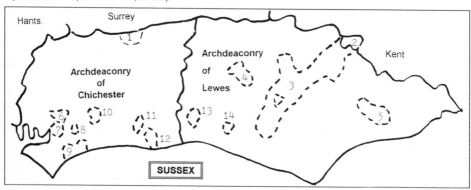

WARWICKSHIRE

The county was split between the Dioceses of Lichfield (the north-eastern part) and Worcester (the south-western). All parishes are listed and their diocese shown *in Tracing Your Ancestors in Warwickshire*, June Watkins and Pauline Saul, 4th edn., Birmingham and Midland S.G.H. (1996), and in the *National Index of Parish Registers* **5** (1966).

Bishop's Transcripts

Records for the **Diocese of Lichfield** are at the *Lichfield Record Office*, Lichfield.
For details see under 'Staffordshire and Derbyshire', page 40.

Records for the **Diocese of Worcester** are at the *Hereford and Worcester Record Office*, County Hall, Worcester.
For details see under 'Worcestershire', page 00. There are microfilms of all BTs in the Diocese of Worcester at the *Warwickshire County Record Office*, Warwick.

Tracing Your Ancestors in Warwickshire and the *National Index* **5** give starting dates and all gaps of four or more years for all parishes in the diocese.

Marriage Licences

Like the BTs, these are in the appropriate record offices for the two **Dioceses of Lichfield** (up to and including 1847 only, although the Archdeaconry of Coventry was transferred to the Diocese of Worcester in 1836); and **Worcester**. They are described on pages 40 and 48.
Also at *Lichfield* are ML records for some Warwickshire peculiars:
Dean and Chapter of Lichfield (Arley, Edgbaston); 1624-1890. Index in progress.
Bishop's Itchington (Chadshunt, Gaydon): 1682-1855. Indexed.
Packwood, 1755-1808 (TS at *Soc. of Gen.*).
Bishop's Tachbrook, 1732-1832.
Merevale, 1767-1862. Ts at *Lichfield Record Office.*
Ufton Decani, 1753-67, 1792-99.

A few marriage bonds for the **Peculiar of Stratford-upon-Avon**, 1618-1621, are at the *Centre for Kentish Studies, Maidstone* (page 26).

For the Diocese of Birmingham (established in 1905, basically comprising the area covered by Warwickshire) *Birmingham Central Library (Archives)* has registers of MLs 1915-88 [BDR/D2/5/1-5] and applications for MLs 1944-95 [BDR/C4/1-64], unlisted.

Microfilm of BTs for Coventry St Michael, 1662-1847, and Coventry St John 1752-1841 is held in *Coventry City Archives*.

See also **Faculty Office** and **Vicar General**'s ML records, pages 7 and 8.

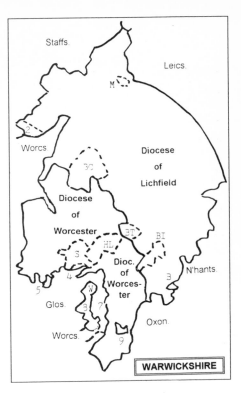

WARWICKSHIRE

Peculiar of Stratford upon Avon (S)
Stratford upon Avon, Bishopton, Bridgetown, Clopton, Dodwell, Drayton, Luddington, Shottery, Welcombe.
Peculiar of Hampton Lucy (HL)
Hampton Lucy, Alveston, Charlecote, Wasperton. Places in these two peculiars also occur in the consistory court of Worcester.
Peculiar of Bishops Itchington (BI)
Bishops Itchington, Chadshunt, Gaydon.
Peculiar of Bishops Tachbrook (BT)
Peculiars of Baddesley Clinton, Barston, Knowle, Packwood and Temple Balsall (BC)
Peculiar of Merevale (M)
Peculiar of Banbury and Cropredy (B)
Mollington.
Peculiar of the Dean and Chapter of Lichfield
Edgbaston (**2**).
Diocese of Gloucester (parishes partly in Glos.)
Welford (**5**), Weston upon Avon (**4**), Sutton-under-Brailes (**9**).
Diocese and County of Worcester (7)
(Worcs. parishes detached)
Alderminster, Shipston on Stour, Tidmington, Tredington.

Warwickshire parishes in the Diocese of Worcester are listed overleaf.

Warwickshire parishes in the diocese of **Worcester**:

Alcester, Gt. Alne, Alveston, Arrow, Aston Cantlow, Atherston on Stour, Barcheston, Barford, Barton on the Heath, Bearley, Beaudesert, Bidford, Billesley, Binton, Brailes, Budbrooke, Burmington, Butlers Marston, Charlecote, Cherington, Claverdon, Long Compton, Compton Verney, Compton Wynyates, Coughton, Eatington, Exhall, Halford, Hampton Lucy, Haseley, Haselor, Hatton, Henley in Arden, Honington, Idlicote, Ilmington (detd. **W8**), Ipsley, Kineton, Kinwarton, Lapworth, Lighthorne, Loxley, Moreton Morrell, Morton Bagot, Newbold Pacey, Norton Lindsey, Oxhill, Pillerton Hersey and Priors, Preston Bagot, Rowington, Salford, Sherbourne, Snitterfield, Spernall, Stratford-upon-Avon, Stretton on the Fosse (detd. **W8**), Studley, Tanworth, Temple Grafton, Tysoe, Ullenhall, Warwick, Wasperton, Weethley, Wellesbourne, Whatcote, Whichford, Whitchurch (detd. **W8**), Wixford, Gt. Wolford, Wolverton, Wootton Wawen, Wroxhall.

WESTMORLAND
(now part of Cumbria)

Cumbria Record Office, Kendal

has BTs for the whole county. See *Cumbrian Ancestors* (Cumbria Archive Service, 2nd edn., 1993, £4.99).

The north-eastern part of the county lay in the Diocese of Carlisle, and the south-western Deaneries of Kendal and Lonsdale were in the Diocese of Chester, Archdeaconry of Richmond.

Bishop's Transcripts

Those for parishes in the **Diocese of Carlisle** date from around 1664, and those in **the Diocese of Chester** from about 1689. Starting and finishing dates (but not gaps) for all parishes are given in *Cumbrian Ancestors*. Microfilm copies of Westmorland BTs are also available at the Carlisle branch of the C.R.O.

Marriage Licences

As for Cumberland, page 15.

For a map of the county, see with Cumberland, page 15.

WILTSHIRE

Wiltshire and Swindon Record Office, Trowbridge

has MLs for Wiltshire and Berkshire and BTs for the whole **Diocese of Salisbury**, which covered Wiltshire and Berkshire. These are described briefly in the booklet *Sources for Wiltshire Family History* (1997) on sale from the Record Office.

Bishop's Transcripts

These are arranged by parish and in general start in the early C17 (but with very occasional BTs from C16). C17 coverage is intermittent, and the series ends in 1880. Surviving years and gaps for each parish are shown in the 7-part series *Location of Documents for Wiltshire Parishes*, Barbara J. Carter, 1981-2 (1 Lansdown Road, Swindon SN1 3NE). See also the *National Index of Parish Registers*, **8**, part 2 (1992).

Marriage Licences

The main **Diocesan** series is complete from 1615 to 1842 except for the Commonwealth period. This covers the whole county, except for peculiars, for which there are separate series. The Diocesan series also includes many Berkshire MLs, but there is also a separate series of Archdeacon's bonds for that county (see pages 10-11).

Although the Archdeacons of Wiltshire and Salisbury do not appear to have issued MLs, there is a sizeable series issued by the **Dean of Salisbury** for many parishes in Wilts., Berks. and Dorset in his Peculiar (listed in part 4 of the Wilts. R.O. Guide, *Records of the Bishop, Archdeacons etc.*, Pamela Stewart, 1974; and also in *Probate Jurisdictions*); and in other small series detailed opposite.

The majority of bonds and allegations to 1823 have been abstracted in some form, as follows:

Bishop's MLs (Wiltshire and Berkshire):
1615-1622, 1626/7-1646, 1660-1682 (published in *The Genealogist* **24-38**);
1622-1626 (omitted from *The Genealogist*) MS (*W. & S. R.O.*);
1682-1700, TS (*W. & S. R.O.* and *Society of Genealogists*);
1700-1734. Index on fiche (in parts), Wilts. F.H.S.
1700-1823, MS (*W. & S. R.O.*, abstracted by Mrs C.E. Whipple, approx. 90,000, currently being corrected by Wilts. F.H.S.).

All these abstracts are arranged primarily by year, and those to 1700 appear to be chronological within each year. From 1700-1823, the arrangement is alphabetical within the year. All abstracts show place of abode for both parties (when given) but not place of marriage.

The other main series of bonds and allegations is for the **Peculiar of the Dean of Salisbury**:
1638-1645, 1672-1686 (published in *Wiltshire Notes & Queries* **6** and **7**, misleadingly described as 'Dean and Chapter' peculiars, but actually mainly 'Dean's' peculiars);
1660-1671, MS (**W. & S. R.O.**);
1687-1699, not abstracted;
1700-1823, MS (**W. & S. R.O.**, similar to Diocesan series, abstracted by Mrs Whipple).
Indexed TS, 1739-1743, at the **Soc. of Gen.** only.

There were a number of small peculiars with ML records *at W. & S. R.O.*:

Dean and Chapter (Bishop's Canning, Bramshaw, Britford, Homington, Southbroom, Stourpaine): 1601-1639, 1661-99 not abstracted; 1702-1823, MS abstract (Mrs Whipple).

Precentor (Westbury with Bratton and Ditton): 1611, 1627-43, 1663-99 (not abstracted); 1702, 1710-1799, MS abstract (Mrs Whipple).

Treasurer (Alderbury with Pitton and Farley, Figheldean, Calne with Berwick Bassett, Blackland and Cherhill): 1663-1669, 1680-99 (not abstracted); 1709-99 MS abstract (Mrs Whipple).

There are a few bonds and allegations for Winterbourne Dauntsey, in the **Peculiar of Chute and Chisenbury**, 1612-1818, not abstracted.

The Vicar of Corsham was entitled to issue MLs within his peculiar (**Corsham**) and there is a series of bonds and MLs 1628-1765 at **W. & S. R.O.** [1285/2 and 3], not abstracted.

For records of peculiars at the **W. & S. R.O.** solely in Berkshire or Dorset, see under those counties.

See also **Faculty Office** and **Vicar General**'s ML records, pages 7 and 8.

Parishes in Wiltshire outside the jurisdiction of the archdeaconries of Salisbury and Wiltshire.

B : Prebend of Bishopstone; **C** : Prebend of Chute and Chisenbury; **CB** : Prebend of Combe (Bisset) and Harnham; **CC** : Peculiar of Castle Combe; **CG** : Consistory Court of Gloucester; **CS** : Consistory Court of Salisbury (in Bishop's Peculiars); **CW** : Consistory and Archdeaconry Courts of Winchester; **D** : Prebend of Durnford; **DC** : Peculiar Court of the Dean of and Chapter of Salisbury; **DS** : Peculiar Court of the Dean of Salisbury; **H** : Prebend of Highworth; **HB** : Prebend of Hurstbourne and Burbage; **N** : Prebend of Netheravon; **P** : Peculiar Court of the Precentor of Salisbury; **SD** : Archdeaconry of the Sub-Dean of Salisbury; **SF** : Peculiar of the Lord Warden of Savernake Forest; **T** : Peculiar of Trowbridge; **TC** : Peculiar Court of the Treasurer in the Prebend of Calne; **VC** : Peculiar of the Perpetual Vicar of Corsham; **W** : Peculiar of the Dean and Canons of Windsor in Wantage; **WW** : Prebend of Wilsford and Woodford.

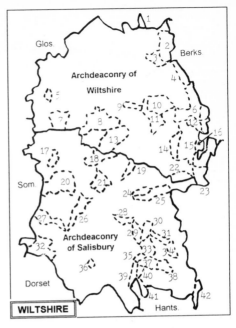

WILTSHIRE

Alderbury **TC38**; Baydon **DS6**; Gt. & Lit. Bedwyn **SF&DS15**; Berwick Bassett **TC9**; Berwick St. James **CS28**; Bishops Cannings **DC13**; Bishopstone **B&DS4**; Blackland (Calne) **TC8**; Bramshaw **DC42**; Bratton (Westbury) **P20**; Britford **DC37**; Broad Blunsdon **H&DS2**; South Broom **DC13**; Burbage **HB&DS14**; Calne **TC8**; Castle Combe **CC5**; Cherhill (Calne) **TC8**; Chisenbury **C&DS24**; Chute **C&DS23**; Collingbourne Ducis **SF&CS22**; Coombe Bissett **CB&DS39**; Corsham **VC&CS7**; (also archd. of Wilts); Devizes **CS18**; Dilton (Westbury) **P20**; Durnford **D&DS30**; Farley **TC34**; Figheldean **TC25**; (West) Harnham **CB&DS35**; Heytesbury **DS26**; Highworth **H&DS2**; Hill Deverill **DS27**; Homington **DC40**; Horningsham **DS27**; Hungerford **W&DS12**; Kingswood **CG** (detd); Knook **DS26**; Lake (Wilsford) **WW&DS19**; West Lavington **CS21**; Marlborough **CS11**; Marston Meysey **CG1**; South Marston **H&DS2**; Mere **DS32**; Milford **SD&CS33**; Netheravon **N&DS24**; Ogbourne St. Andrew and St. George **W&DS10**; Pitton **TC34**; Potterne **CS18**; Preshute **CS11**; Ramsbury **DS6**; Salisbury **SD&CS33**; Salisbury Close **DS33**; Sevenhampton **H&DS2**; Shalbourne **W&DS16**; Southbroom **DC13**; Staverton (Trowbridge) **CS&T17**; Stert **CS18**; Stratford-sub-Castle **SD&CS33**; Stratton St. Margaret **VC&CS3** (also arch of Wilts); Swallowcliffe **DS36**; Trowbridge **CS&T17**; Tytherington (Heytesbury) **DS26**; West Wellow **CW42**; Westbury **P20**; Whitsbury or Whichbury **CW41**; Wilsford **WW&DS19**; Winterbourne Dauntsey **C&DS31**; Woodford **WW&DS29**.

WORCESTERSHIRE

(now part of Hereford and Worcester; northern tip in West Midlands county).

Almost all of Worcestershire was in **the Diocese of Worcester**, whose records are at the

Hereford and Worcester Record Office, County Hall, Worcester.

Bishop's Transcripts

Starting dates and gaps of four or five years are given for all parishes in the *National Index of Parish Registers* **5** (1966). In that (pp. 255-7), the vicissitudes affecting arrangement of the BTs are explained. At the *Record Office* there is a master guide to all parishes showing exactly what years survive for each parish, and appropriate references.

The BTs have been filmed by the Mormons, so baptisms and marriages should appear in the I.G.I. Microfilms of BTs for the Diocese are also at the **Warwickshire County Record Office**, *Warwick.*

Most BTs start about 1610, and to 1700 are arranged according to parish. From that date on, to 1838, they remain in the original arrangement, by year, and, within each year, by Deanery. They include Warwickshire parishes in the Diocese and those in Peculiars, not markedly more irregular than elsewhere.

Parishes in the north-west of the county are in the **Diocese of Hereford**, with records at the *Hereford Record Office*, page 23. The parishes are: Abberley, Bayton, Bockleton, Clifton-on-Teme, Eastham, Edvin Loach, Hanley Child and William,

Knighton-on-Teme, Kyre Magna and Parva, Lindridge, Mamble, Orleton, Pensax, Rock, Lower Sapey, Stanford-on-Teme, Stockton-on-Teme, Tenbury.

For 17 parishes in the **Diocese of Gloucester** (some formerly in Gloucestershire), see under 'Gloucestershire', pages 21-22, for BTs and MLs, and the *National Index* **5**, for original dioceses.

Marriage Licences

These records are also at the main (County Hall) **Worcester Record Office**. For the pre-Commonwealth records, 1553-1645, there is a MS calendar and index. MLs are also listed in the published calendar to probate records, 1544-1600, British Record Society **31**. Otherwise, from 1660 ML records including C18 and C19 contemporary registers are generally arranged by year. Name indexes have been compiled for the period 1720-1730 and for 1871-1916. See 'Worcester Diocesan Marriage Licences in the mid-18th century', Ruth Piggott, *Midland Ancestor* **10.**1 (Sept. 1992).

For parishes in the **Diocese of Hereford**, see under 'Herefordshire', page 23

See also Faculty Office and Vicar General's ML records, pages 7 and 8.

Worcestershire parishes, detached from the main county, or in peculiars, but still also in the jurisdiction of the **Consistory Court of Worcester**; and those in the jurisdiction of the Consistory Court of Hereford.

Detached parishes in the diocese of Worcester:
Alderminster **10**; Blockley **16**; Daylesford **19**; Dudley **1**; Evenlode **18**; Shipston on Stour **14**; Tidmington **14**.

Peculiars (also subject to the Consistory Court of Worcester):
Alvechurch **3**; Berrow **15**; Bradbury **9**; Bredon **13**; Bredons Norton **13**; Cutsdean **17**; Fladbury **9**; Hanbury **5**; Hartlebury **4**; Holdfast **12**; Kempsey **8**; Norton (nr. Bredon) **13**; Norton (nr. Kempsey) **8**; Queenhill **12**; Ripple **12**; Stock **9**; Stoulton **8**; Throckmorton **9**; Tibberton **6**; Tredington **11**; Wolverley **2**; Worcester, College Precincts and St. Michael in Bedwardine **7**; Wyre Piddle **9**.

Parishes and chapelries in the diocese of Hereford:
Abberley, Bayton, Bockleton, Clifton on Teme, Eastham, Edvin Loach, Hanley Child and William, Knighton-on-Teme, Kyre Magna and Parva, Lindridge, Mamble, Orleton, Pensax, Rock, Lower Sapey, Stanford-on-Teme, Tenbury.

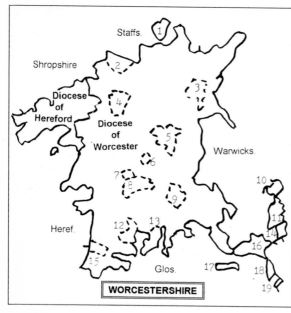

Staffs.
Shropshire
Diocese of Hereford
Diocese of Worcester
Warwicks.
Heref.
Glos.
WORCESTERSHIRE

YORKSHIRE

Most of Yorkshire was in the Diocese of York. The exceptions were parts of the West and North Ridings forming part of the Archdeaconry of Richmond, and parishes in the Peculiar jurisdictions of Northallertonshire and Crayke.

All BTs and MLs for the Diocese of York (except Nottinghamshire) are at the

Borthwick Institute of Historical Research, York.

Bishop's Transcripts

The Institute issues an introductory leaflet, and full details of BTs for all parishes are given in the Borthwick *Institute Handlist of Parish Register Transcripts*, N.K.M.Gurney, 1976 (o.p.).

The series begins about 1600 but there are only a few pre-Commonwealth BTs. They continued until the mid-C19, decreasing in numbers (and no marriages) after 1837; those for parishes in the Diocese of Ripon after 1836 are at **Leeds District Archives**. BTs are arranged by parish and are consulted on microfilm. Photocopies of BTs of some parishes are at **York City Library**.

Microfilm copies of BTs are at:

Barnsley Central Library: Ardsley, Askham Bryan, Barnsley, Bolton upon Dearne, Cawthorne, Cumberworth, Darfield, Darton, Old Edlington, Elsecar, Felkirk, Gawber, High Hoyland, Hoyland Nether, Monk Bretton, Penistone, Royston, Silkstone, Tankersley, Thrybergh, Thurgoland, Thurnscoe, Wath upon Dearne, Wentworth, Woolley, Worsbrough, and Wortley.

Calderdale District Archives, Halifax: Elland, Halifax, Hartshead, Heptonstall, Luddenden, Ripponden, Sowerby, Todmorden and twelve post-1812 parishes.

Doncaster Archives. Microfilm of BTs for about 45 parishes in Doncaster Archdeaconry as well as a few parishes outside it.

East Riding of Yorkshire Archive Office, Beverley: nearly 100 parishes in the administrative area of the present authority, also to include some from parishes in the East Riding Archdeaconry. where the earliest original registers have not survived.

Sheffield Archives, Sheffield: all 104 parishes now in the county of South Yorkshire.

The western half of the North Riding and the northern tip of the West Riding were in the **Arch-deaconry of Richmond**, with records now at the

Leeds District Archives (West Yorkshire Archives Service), Sheepscar, Leeds.

These comprise about 342 parishes or chapelries, with a fairly continuous series of BTs from 1674 on; occasional returns for some parishes survive for earlier years, the earliest 1613. A leaflet listing parishes and covering dates is available.

Durham University Library Archives and Special Collections, Palace Green Section, Durham

has BTs for the peculiar jurisdictions of **Crayke** (to 1837) and **Allertonshire** (to 1813): Birkby, Brompton, Cowesby, Deighton, Hutton Bonville, Kirby Sigston, Leake, Northallerton with Romanby, Osmotherley, North Otterington, West Rounton, Nether Silton, Thornton-le-Street, High Worsall. See *Durham Diocesan Records: Summary List of BTs* for dates.

Marriage Licences

In the C19 abbreviated notes were made by William Paver from marriage licence registers which have since disappeared. These notes have been published by the Yorkshire Archaeological Society: 1567-1630, vols. 7-20, with consolidated index, Extra Series **2**; 1630-1644 (*40*); 1660-1674 (*43*); 1674-1514 (*46*).

MLs in these volumes, and for the main collection of bonds at the Borthwick Institute, which survive from 1660, are for the whole northern **Province of York**, not just the Diocese. From 1715 on these are in annual bundles (to 1837 sorted alphabetically by groom's surname). The Institute is publishing indexes from 1839 back by decades (1735-49, intervening decades, 1830-39, to date). 'Sede vacante' MLs for 1776-77 are published in the *Northern Genealogist* **3** and **4**. An index to 'Sede vacante' bonds and allegations 1660, 1664, 1683, 1686-68, 1761, 1776-77, 1807-08, 1847 and 1860 is available at the Institute.

In addition to the main series of bonds and allegations, there are ML records of the following peculiars at the **Borthwick Institute**:

Hexham and Hexhamshire (see under Durham and Northumberland, page 19);

Acomb 1714-1863 (published in *Borthwick Institute Bulletin* **2**: 3 (1981);

Alne and Tollerton 1782-1865;

Bishop Wilton 1699-1865;

South Cave 1793-1865;

Howden and Howdenshire 1709-1865 (indexed; this was a peculiar of the Dean and Chapter of Durham, and comprised Howden, Asselby, Barlby, Barmby Marsh, Blacktoft, Brantingham, Eastrington, Ellerker, Hemingbrough, Holtby, Laxton, Skipwith, Walkington and Welton. The records are at York through an historical accident);

Selby (including Brayton, Barlow, Burn, Gateforth, Hambleton, Thorpe Willoughby) 1664-1868 (index 1664-1710, Y.A.S. R.S. **47**);

Snaith (including Airmyn, Balne, Carlton, Cowick, Goole, Gowdall, Heck, Hensall, Hook, Ousefleet, Pollington, Rawcliffe, Reedness, Swinefleet, Whitgift) 1629-1789.

Dean and Chapter of York. Bonds, 1613-1879 (56 boxes), few from early C17. Published index 1613-1839 by E.B. and W.R. Newsome (York F.H.S., 1985, can be purchased from the Institute). The extensive jurisdiction includes in Yorkshire: Aldborough, Boston Spa, Bramham, Brotherton, Burton Leonard and Pidsea, Copmanthorpe, Dunsthorpe, Helperby, Helperthorpe, Hornby, Luttons Ambo, Upper Poppleton, Weaverthorpe, Wharram le Street and 14 York city parishes.

Two boxes of odd ML records for Allertonshire are at *Durham University Library Archives and Special Collections*. These consist of bonds and allegations for 1667, 1732-34, 1749, 1756-58, 1760-66, 1769, 1774-75, 1777-84, 1786-90, 1796-1808, 1812, 1819, 1823-30, 1875-81. There are also a few Allertonshire documents in the main series of Durham marriage bonds and allegations (see page 19).

MLs for the *Archdeaconry of Richmond* are at the *Leeds District Archives*. They extend from 1628 to 1823 (mostly post-1700), consisting in part of complete annual bundles and some fragments from collapsed bundles. Index now completed. Register of licences, 1777-1790.

Rossington, Austerfield in Blyth, part of Bawtry, chapelry of Hardworth, Auckley and Blaxton, chapelries of Finningley, were all in the **Archdeaconry of Nottingham** - so for records see under 'Nottinghamshire', page 36.

See also **Faculty Office** ML records, page 7.

THE PROVINCE OF YORK

Apart from the areas listed below,

Cheshire was in the diocese of Chester;
Cumberland was in the diocese of Carlisle;
Durham was in the diocese of Durham;
Flintshire (southern detachment) was in the diocese of Chester;
Lancashire was in the diocese of Chester;
Northumberland was in the diocese of Durham;
Nottinghamshire was in the diocese of York;
Westmorland was in the diocese of Carlisle;
Yorkshire (all Ridings and the Ainsty of York [13]) was in the diocese of York;

In **Cumberland** the deanery of Copeland (3) was in the western division of the consistory court of the archdeaconry of Richmond (diocese of Chester), and the parish of Alston (2) was in the diocese of Durham.

In **Denbighshire** the parish of Holt (16) was in the diocese of Chester.

In **Flintshire** the peculiar of Hawarden (15) was in the diocese of Chester.

In **Lancashire** that part of the county north of the River Ribble (5 and 10) was in the western division of the consistory court of the archdeaconry of Richmond (diocese of Chester); and Aighton, Chaigley and Bailey (14) were in the diocese of York.

In **Northumberland** the peculiar of Hexham and Hexhamshire (1) was in the jurisdiction of the archbishop of York until 1837; and Tockerington (Throckrington) (1) was a prebend of York.

In **Westmorland** the deaneries of Kendal and Lonsdale (6) were in the western division of the consistory court of the archdeaconry of Richmond (diocese of Chester).

In **Yorkshire, North Riding,** the deaneries of Richmond and Catterick (8) were in the eastern division of the consistory court of the archdeaconry of Richmond (diocese of Chester); the parish of Sockburn (4), the peculiar of Crayke (12) until 1837, and the bishop of Durham's peculiar of Allertonshire (9) until 1846 fell within the jurisdiction of the consistory court of Durham; and the parishes of Brompton, Deighton, High Worsall, Kirby Sigston; Northallerton and West Rounton (9) formed the peculiar of Allerton and Allertonshire under the jurisdiction of the dean and chapter of Durham until 1846.

In **Yorkshire, West Riding,** the deanery of Lonsdale (7) was in the western division of the archdeaconry of Richmond (diocese of Chester); the deanery of Boroughbridge (11) was in the eastern division.

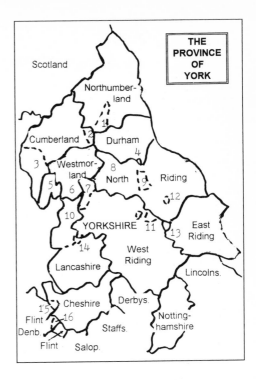

THE PROVINCE OF YORK

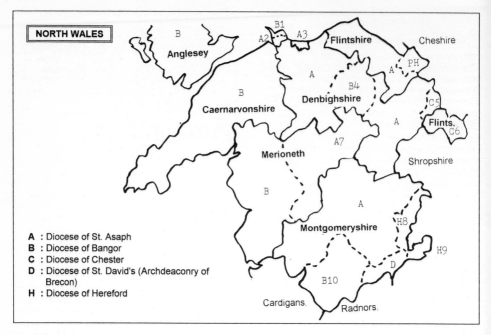

NORTH WALES

B — Anglesey

B1, A2, A3 — Flintshire — Cheshire

A — PH — A

B — Caernarvonshire — Denbighshire — B4 — C5

A — Flints. — C6

A7 — Merioneth — Shropshire

B

A

Montgomeryshire — H8

B10 — H9

D

Cardigans. — Radnors.

A : Diocese of St. Asaph
B : Diocese of Bangor
C : Diocese of Chester
D : Diocese of St. David's (Archdeaconry of Brecon)
H : Diocese of Hereford

Caernarvonshire
Llandudno **B1**; Eglwys-Rhos **A2**; Llangystennin **A2**; Llysfaen **A3**;

Denbighshire (B4)
Clocaenog, Derwen, Efenechtid, Gyffylliog, Llanbedr, Dyffryn Clwyd, Llandyrnog, Llanelidan, Llanfair Dyffryn Clwyd, Llanfywrog, Llangwyfan, Llangynhafal, Llanhychan, Llanrhaeadr-yng-Nghinmeirch, Llan-rhudd, Llanynys, Ruthin; Holt **C5**.

Flintshire
Peculiar of Hawarden (**PH**);
Southern Detachment (**C6**):
Bangor Iscoed, Hanmer, Overton, Threapwood, Worthenbury.

Merionethshire (A7)
Betws Gwerful Goch, Corwen, Gwyddelwern, Llandderfel, Llandrillo, Llanfor, Llangar, Llangywer, Llansanffraid Glyndyfrdwy, Llanymawddwy, Llanuwchllyn, Llanycil, Mallwyd.

Montgomeryshire
Alberbury (partly Salop) **H8**; Buttington **H8**; Carno **B10**; Churchstoke **H9**; Forden **H8**; Hyssington **H9**; Kerry (Ceri) **D**; Llandinam **B10**; Llangurig **B10**; Llanidloes **B10**; Llanwynog **B10**; Mainstone (partly Salop) **H9**; Mochdre **D**; Montgomery **H8**; Penstrowed **B10**; Snead **H9**; Trefeglwys **B10**; Worthen (partly Salop) **H8**.

For the Episcopal Consistory Court of Hereford (with jurisdiction over nine parishes in Montgomeryshire) see *Hereford Record Office*, page 23.

WALES

The six counties comprising **North Wales** (Anglesey, Caernarvon, Denbigh, Flint, Merioneth and Montgomery) were mainly in the Dioceses of Bangor or St. Asaph.

In **South Wales**, Glamorgan and Monmouth were mainly in the Diocese of Llandaff, whilst the Diocese of St David's comprised the remainder (Brecknock, Carmarthen, Cardigan, Pembroke and Radnor).

The records of all four dioceses are at the

National Library of Wales, Department of Manuscripts and Records, Aberystwyth.

Bishop's Transcripts

Dates of surviving BTs for all Welsh parishes are given in *Parish Registers of Wales* by C.J. Williams and J. Watts-Williams (N.L.W. and Welsh County Archivists' Group with Society of Genealogists, *National Index of Parish Registers* **13**, 1986). BTs are arranged by parish.

All BTs at the N.L.W. have been microfilmed by the Mormons, and so baptisms and marriages should appear in the I.G.I.

Bangor: 9 parishes from 1660s, fair number from 1670s, to second half of C19. The schedule notes 'There are about 200 transcripts which are illegible, fragmentary or otherwise unidentifiable'.

Wales: BTs continued

St. Asaph: 28 parishes from 1662; most end c.1830-1860. Gaps in most sets, but a few have apparently complete runs (e.g. Guilsfield 1667-1859, Llangynyw 1662-1839). Most gaps fairly small and coverage seems to be good. Microfilm of parishes in Denbighs., Flints. and Merioneth are at *Denbighshire (Ruthin)* and *Flintshire (Hawarden) Record Offices*; parishes and covering dates are listed in *Clwyd F.H.S.* Journal **5** (Winter 1981).

Llandaff: 62 parishes have BTs for 1696, but then mainly a gap until 1720s. In general end 1860-1890. Some gaps in sets, but usually for early decades of C18; otherwise coverage good. There are six MS vols. containing alphabetical indexes for the whole diocese for the years 1813, 1814, 1815.
Microfilms of parishes in Glamorgan up to 1837 are available at the *Glamorgan Record Office, Cardiff,* and of West Glamorgan parishes in Llandaff Diocese at the *West Glamorgan Record Office, Swansea;* also at *Gwent Record Office, Cwmbran,* for three Brecons. parishes, Crickhowell, Llangatwg and Llanfihangel Cwm Du, 1797-1809, and for Llanmartin, Mon., 1725-1839.

St. David's: One at 1662, then a fair number from 1670s or late C17, to late C19. Gaps in all sets, often considerable, and records are very sparse for all C18 and up to 1811/2.

Swansea and Brecon (formerly part of St. David's). Five parishes begin in 1671, otherwise starting dates vary from late C17 to early C18; generally terminating c.1830-1880. Small gaps in nearly all sets, but for no specific period; coverage quite good. Microfilms of parishes in Glamorgan up to 1837 are available at the *West Glamorgan Record Office, Swansea.*

Exceptions: Holt and Isycoed, Denbighs.; and Bangor, Hanmer, Overton, Worthenbury in Flints. (southern detachment) were in the **Diocese of Chester**, BTs at *Cheshire Record Office*, page 13.
Welsh parishes in the **Diocese of Hereford**, *Hereford Record Office*, page 23:
Montgomerys.: Alderbury, Buttington, Churchstoke, Forden, Hyssington, Mainstone, Montgomery, Snead, Worthen;
Monmouths.: Dixton Newton, Monmouth;
Radnors.: Knighton, Michaelchurch-on-Arrow, Norton, Presteign, Old and New Radnor.

Marriage Licences

Bonds and affidavits for the four dioceses are all at the *National Library of Wales* and there is a computerised index up to 1837 (leaflet available). They have been microfilmed by the Mormons so should appear in the I.G.I.

Bangor: ML records effectively only survive from 1760, arranged chronologically.
St. Asaph: The series effectively starts in 1690, continuing until 1938, chronological arrangement.
Llandaff: Filed for the following years: 1665, 1670-1672, 1674-76, 1680-82, 1693, 1707-08, 1733 on (except 1741) to 1941. Arranged chronologically.
St. David's: Starting 1661, and few for late C17 and early C18. Divided into two main sections. Documents relating to present **Diocese of Swansea and Brecon**, 1661-1867, arranged chronologically according to parish in bound volumes. All others arranged chronologically within the sequence. For published abstracts, C17 and C18, see *West Wales Historical Records* 3-12.

For parishes in the **Diocese of Chester**, see p.13; and for those in the **Diocese of Hereford**, see p.23.

See also **Faculty Office** and **Vicar General**'s ML records, pages 7 and 8.

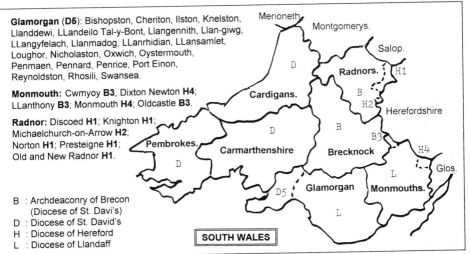

Glamorgan (D5): Bishopston, Cheriton, Ilston, Knelston, Llanddewi, LLandeilo Tal-y-Bont, Llangennith, Llan-giwg, LLangyfelach, Llanmadog, LLanrhidian, LLansamlet, Loughor, Nicholaston, Oxwich, Oystermouth, Penmaen, Pennard, Penrice, Port Einon, Reynoldston, Rhosili, Swansea.

Monmouth: Cwmyoy **B3**, Dixton Newton **H4**; LLanthony **B3**; Monmouth **H4**; Oldcastle **B3**.

Radnor: Discoed **H1**; Knighton **H1**; Michaelchurch-on-Arrow **H2**; Norton **H1**; Presteigne **H1**; Old and New Radnor **H1**.

B : Archdeaconry of Brecon (Diocese of St. Davi's)
D : Diocese of St. David's
H : Diocese of Hereford
L : Diocese of Llandaff

SOUTH WALES

53

IRELAND

Note: I am grateful to Mr Michael Leader for contributing the introduction to this section. Most details of published indexes are taken, by kind permission, from *Marriage Licences: Abstracts and Indexes in the Society of Genealogists*, compiled by Lydia Collins, 3rd ed., 1987. I am also grateful to Mr Anthony Camp for drawing my attention to the important published indexes to Dublin ML records.

There are no longer Bishop's Transcripts in Ireland. However, if the searcher is extremely fortunate, a copy of the registers of the parish he is interested in may have been made by the then incumbent prior to the originals being sent to Dublin for 'safe keeping'. The accuracy of these copies, which are normally not included in lists of extant registers, must occasionally be open to question as indeed must any copy of any parish register anywhere. These fortuitous documents are, in effect, a Bishop's Transcript, in reverse.

Most original **Marriage Licence Bonds** were destroyed in the Public Record Office of Ireland during the civil war in Ireland in 1922. However, indexes to all dioceses, except for Derry, are in the **National Archives of Ireland** in Dublin, though cannot be considered a complete record. In the *N.A.I.*, abstracts of many of the original bonds, taken before 1922, are card-indexed, and give full genealogical data included in the originals. The Thrift Collection and Sir William Betham's abstracts from Dublin Bonds are particularly valuable. The latter are on microfilm at the *Society of Genealogists*.

In Ireland, Licences were only taken out for marriages when both of the parties were members of the Church of Ireland. But, after 1746, they included mixed marriages. Nevertheless, occasionally one finds a marriage by Licence between two Roman Catholics in a Protestant parish register celebrated by the Church of Ireland incumbent.

General Jurisdiction

Prerogative Court of Armagh: Act books, 1748-1751 (57th Report of the Deputy Keeper of Public Records in Ireland, 1929-30, Appendix).

Betham's abstracts, 1629-1810. Original transcripts in *N.A.I.* Microfilm of Betham's notebooks at *Society of Genealogists*.

Local (Consistory) Jurisdictions

Clonfert: Index 1739, 1815-45, extracts of a few bonds at *N.A.I.* (Supplement to *The Irish Ancestor*, 1970).

Cloyne: Index, 1630-1800 (published, by George T. Green, 1899/1900).

Cork and Ross: Index, 1630-1750 (published by Herbert Webb Gillman, 1896/7).

Dublin: Published index (with probate records) 1638-1648 (C-Z), 1661-72, June 1701 - Jan. 1702, Nov. 1703 - Nov. 1706, 1746-1800, and, in Addenda, 1638-48 (A-B), 1672-1713, 1741-46 (from Betham MSS.) (*Appendix to 26th Report of the Deputy Keeper of Public Records, 1895* - published 1894, XLV Part 2); 1800 - Apr. 1856 (Appendix to *30th Report, 1899* - published 1900, XLIV).

Bonds, 1749-1813 (*57th Report of the Deputy Keeper of Public Records in Ireland, 1929-30*, Appendix).

Betham's notebooks, 1638-1824 (original transcripts at *N.A.I.*; microfilm at *Society of Genealogists*).

Killaloe: Bonds 1680-1720, 1760-62 (*The Irish Genealogist*, **5**, 5, Nov. 1978, pp. 580-90); Act book 1776-1845 (*I.G.*, **5**, 6, Nov. 1979, pp. 710-19; also *57th Report of the Deputy Keeper of Public Records in Ireland, 1929-30*, Appendix).

Ossory: Bonds, 1669-1823, extracts (*The Irish Genealogist*, **4**, 4, Nov. 1971, pp. 331-41). 'Licences', 1739-1804 (*I.G.* 1990).

Raphoe: Index to bonds, extracts, 1710-55, 1817-1830, held at *N.A.I.* pre-1922 (Supplement to *The Irish Ancestor*, 1969).

Thrift abstracts: Various courts, C17-C19, published in *57th Report of the Deputy Keeper, 1929-30*, Appendix.

NORTHERN IRELAND

Donegal
Raphoe
Londonderry
Derry
Connor·
Antrim
Tyrone
L. Neagh
Armagh
Down
Fermanagh
Clogher
Armagh
Down
Dromore
Newry
Monaghan
Kilmore
Leitrim
Cavan
Louth
Ardagh
Long-ford
Meath

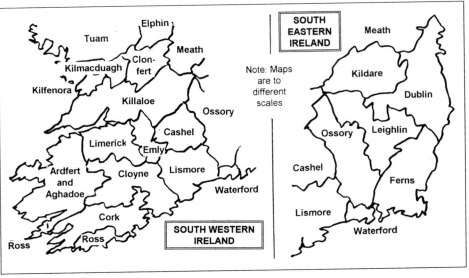

Elphin
Tuam
Meath
Clon-fert
Kilmacduagh
Kilfenora
Killaloe
Ossory
Cashel
Limerick
Emly
Ardfert and Aghadoe
Cloyne
Lismore
Waterford
Cork
Ross
Ross

Note: Maps are to different scales

SOUTH EASTERN IRELAND

Meath
Kildare
Dublin
Ossory
Leighlin
Cashel
Ferns
Lismore
Waterford

SOUTH WESTERN IRELAND

ISLE OF MAN

House of Keys and Registry Office, Deemsters Walk, Douglas, Isle of Man.

Bishop's Transcripts

1734-67, 1786-on (apparently including all C19). Microfilm copies for 1734-67, 1786-99 are at the **Manx National Heritage Library**, *Manx Musum, Kingswood Grove, Douglas*. See *The Manx Family Tree*, Janet Narsimham, 1986.

Marriage Licences

No records survive.